# Women at Work

Chris Aldred teaches and organizes classes for the North of Scotland District of the Workers' Educational Association. She is particularly interested in education for women, and has taught on a wide range of trade union courses. She is an active trade unionist and has been involved in the women's movement for ten years.

**Pan Trade Union Studies**

*also available in this series*

C. Baker and P. Caldwell:
Unions and Change Since 1945

P. Burns and M. Doyle:
Democracy at Work

A. Campbell and J. McIlroy:
Getting Organized

D. Eva and R. Oswald:
Health and Safety at Work

*Series editors*

Peter Caldwell
Tutor/Organizer
Workers' Educational Association
West Midlands

Alan Campbell
Lecturer in Industrial Relations
University of Liverpool

Mel Doyle
Assistant Secretary
Workers' Educational Association

Pan
Trade Union
Studies

# Women at Work

## Chris Aldred

Pan Original
Pan Books   London and Sydney

First published 1981 by Pan Books Ltd,
Cavaye Place, London SW10 9PG
© Chris Aldred and the Workers'
Educational Association 1981
ISBN 0 330 26479 6
Phototypeset by Input Typesetting Ltd,
London SW19 8DR
Printed and bound in Great Britain by
Richard Clay (The Chaucer Press) Ltd,
Bungay, Suffolk

## About the series

This series of books has been written for several groups of people
– those thinking of joining a union, or new members; those who
are just becoming active members; new and less experienced
shop-stewards; and indeed anyone interested in trade unions
today. It aims to provide an introduction to the principles of basic
trade unionism by discussing a wide range of arguments and
issues in the five key areas covered by the books. In
straightforward language each book points the way towards the
action that must be taken by individual trade unionists and by the
movement as a whole if their goals are to be achieved.

## About this book

This book is concerned with the trade union problems which
confront women, and discusses some of the ways of dealing with
these problems through changes at work, at home, and in the
trade unions. It is intended for trade unionists who would like to
see women getting a better deal at work, and for women who are
trying to work out how the trade unions could help women to
fight for improvements in their own lives. Have legal changes
helped women? What have women trade unionists achieved in
the past? Can women ever get fair treatment at work in a society
which still regards women as second class citizens? Do women
take any interest in trade unions? What should trade unions be
doing about the issues which affect women? This book doesn't
answer these questions – that's up to you – but it does provide
some of the background to them, and suggest ways in which
answers might be found.

I would like to dedicate this book to my mother, **Primrose Aldred**, for teaching me to think for myself.

# Acknowledgements

It's difficult to know who to thank first – the women in the Women's Movement who helped me to understand women's oppression, or the trade union students, women and men, who put these ideas into the practical context of everyday trade union life, and developed them further. I must also thank the friends and colleagues who have patiently advised and argued with me, and the North of Scotland District of the Workers' Educational Association, for whom I work – I have learnt a lot by teaching for the WEA. Julia Thomas, who typed the manuscript for me, deserves special thanks – her caustic comments on the carbon copies changed the final version of the book. The staff of Aberdeen City Libraries spent ages chasing up books, pamphlets and other information for me – and then had to chase me to return it all. Lastly, thanks to the editors of this series for their hard work and useful comments.

# Contents

# Introduction

This book is about women and the trade unions. I hope it will give you some new information, new ideas, or new arguments to think about and to use – whether you are a female trade unionist, a male trade unionist, or someone interested in the unions – and some idea of the part trade unions can play in changing life for women.

We often hear that women are not interested in unions. I don't think this is true. 'Apathy' is a nice convenient excuse we can always use to explain why there is no point in us bothering to think or organize around a range of issues. But can we be sure that it is simply a lack of interest among women? Might it be that the trade union movement has simply not put enough effort into informing and educating potential women members and activitists? Perhaps the movement also needs to inform and educate itself?

To work out what we should do we have to look carefully at the kinds of work women do, the education and training girls and women get, and at the work women have to do at home – the second, unpaid job. We have to know what the trade unions can do to improve things for women. We will be looking at these issues in Chapters one and two and hopefully setting the scene for the rest of the book.

The third chapter will look at what the law can do for women. We have all heard by now that we have 'equality' but have we? Is the law able to change the position of women? Is it working properly? Why did trade unions want a change in the law in the first place? These are all questions we will try to answer.

The next question, of course is 'What are we going to do about it?' Trade union organization may need to be changed if we are genuinely keen to involve more women. It has already been affected by the massive growth in women's membership of trade unions in the 1970s. About one in three trade unionists are women. Would you have thought that from the way the trade unions appear when you see national conferences on television, or even from the way you think about trade unions yourself? Chapter four talks about practical changes in the way we organize, and runs through some of the recent developments in the unions.

The fifth chapter goes on to look at a problem which is a bit more difficult to describe, let alone change. It's the problem people talk about when they say 'Women are their own worst enemies'. Sometimes women just don't *want* to get involved in unions. Why not? Is it the fault of the women themselves, or is it something wrong with the unions? If the latter then there is more at issue than just the involvement of women. Not only women, but men as well, may not *want* to get involved, and if we don't tackle this problem, our whole movement will be in danger.

In the last chapter we will look for some positive ideas as to what can be done. We will also take a quick glance at how much women have achieved in the past – something we tend to forget.

I hope you will enjoy reading this book, and that it may sometimes help you to argue a better case for women with your workmates, in your union branch, in your local community groups and, perhaps, even at home! I have found that writing it all down has helped me to see my own point of view more clearly – I hope I will be arguing better too.

One last point. I am a woman, a trade unionist, and I live in Scotland. These are all things that profoundly affect my life, and the way I see things. When you are reading this book, I hope you will agree with me when I speak about issues from a trade union point of view – that is how I see them. I hope too, that if you are a woman, you will find it a nice change to find a book about trade unions which addresses itself to you, rather than leaving you to tag along trying to follow arguments that are obviously based on men's experience. If you are a man, I hope you will understand *why* I have written the book like this – if you feel as if I am not paying as much attention to male readers as I should, perhaps this will show you how women sometimes feel when reading other books about trade unions. Lastly, as I said, I live in Scotland. I am infuriated by books which refer to Scotland and Scottish problems in footnotes, or which ignore us by referring to England, Britain and the UK as if they all meant the same thing. Perhaps Scottish trade unionists deserve a break too!

# Chapter One

## Do women do the same work as men?

'everyone knows':
WOMEN CAN'T LIFT HEAVY WEIGHTS....

Thanks to Caz

... MEN CAN

It's pretty difficult to come to any conclusions about women in the trade unions without knowing what kind of work women do. A line from the song by Jean Hart reprinted on page 18 gives you one idea of what women's work is like: 'He says you're suited to the job – which means the job is boring.' Is that the way you would describe women's paid work? In this chapter we will be looking at the kinds of jobs women do, and why; we will also try to discover the ways in which women's jobs differ from men's, and if this makes any difference to things that trade unions can do.

# The boss's darling

This was written by Jean Hart of the Women's Theatre Group for their play 'Work to Role' about women's employment.

Now come along girls to the factory
The production line is turning
If you work all day for the minimum pay
God knows what you'll be earning
Get stuck in when you arrive
To keep your family alive
At the end of the week you'll just survive
To be the boss's darling.

Your patience and dexterity
He's endlessly adoring
He says you're suited to the job
Which means the job is boring
You think you're earning equal pay
But he has found a million ways
To keep you bottom of the heap OK
'Cos you're the boss's darling

The boss he loves you well, you bet,
He knows that you'll by loyal
You're a breeding ground for the working man
And a resting place from toil
You have no time for the union,
You leave that kind of thing to men,
You're a second class worker and a mother hen
That's why you're the boss's darling.

We'll come along down to the factory
We'll keep you on your toeses
There's lots of unemployment now,
So don't look down your noses
There's shi(f)t work here and shi(f)t work there,
What you do with your family's your affair,
'Cos if you don't like it, there's plenty more
To be the boss's darling

These days we're getting organized,
This time we won't be beaten.
It's 'You lend me a hand with the frying pan,
I'm off to a union meeting.'
You men who cross our picket line,
Remember you'll get yours in time –
The enemy's the same, it's yours and mine,
The scab is the bosses' darling.

In the first part of the chapter we will be looking at whether there really are such things as 'men's work' and 'women's work', and if not, what sort of jobs are more likely to be done by either sex. In the second part of the chapter we will try to decide whether men and women have different skills and talents and, if they do, why, and what effect this has on the jobs they get.

If men and women do different jobs will this cause any difficulties within the trade union movement? Are there any problems in your own union which might be a result of the male members doing different jobs from the women? Or are there hardly any women *in* your union? Or hardly any men? Let's keep these questions in mind, but have a look first of all at whether men and women do different jobs.

What is it that distinguishes women's work from men's work, if anything? Let's see if we can get a clue by looking at a list of jobs, and trying to say if each job is likely to be done by a man, a woman, or by either. You might like to note down what you decide so that you can look back at your ideas again later. Anyway, here is the list.

| | |
|---|---|
| van driver | lorry driver |
| nurse | sewing machinist |
| shop assistant | clerical worker |
| electrician | sales manager |
| teacher | cleaner |
| assembly line worker in electronics | fish filleter |
| assembly line worker in the car industry | dustman |

How did you make up your mind which jobs were likely to be done by men and which by women? Let's see what happens when we try to divide jobs up into 'men's work' and 'women's work'. We all have an idea about what jobs are usually done by men or by women. We often explain this away with reasons like 'men do the dirty jobs'. Let's have a look at some of the things which we say marks out a job as 'men's work' or 'women's work' (you will want to add more to each list).

| Men's work | Women's work |
|---|---|
| ● dirty | ● needs ability to |
| ● requires physical strength | concentrate on |
| ● involves night work | monotonous work |
| ● technical/skilled | ● needs dexterity |
| | ● uses domestic skills |
| | ● semi-skilled |

Do these explanations really work when we look at them closely? Does driving a lorry actually involve dirtier work than driving a van? Or more physical strength? Or longer hours? It's certainly better paid! So is bus driving, as one woman in Aberdeen knows.

Katrina used to drive vans for commercial firms. She likes driving but found that her wages as a van driver were rotten compared to the earnings of bus and lorry drivers. Most van drivers were women and very young men. Bus and lorry drivers in Aberdeen were all men. Katrina pestered the Transport Department until they eventually took her on as a trainee in 1978. As she says, 'It was the only way I could get a reasonably well paid driving job.'

Over the last ten years women have earned just over two-thirds of what men earn *per hour* (so that it's not just that women work less hours for their wage).

So low pay is a key factor in distinguishing women's work. Just take two examples (see Figures 1 and 2). If, in 1975, you looked at those who earned less than £1 per hour you would find this constituted 8 per cent of male manual workers, 52 per cent of full-time female manual workers, and 69 per cent of part-time women manual workers. In 1979, 43 per cent of women working full time earned more than £60 per week, compared with 87 per cent of working men.

But low pay probably isn't what you were thinking about when you described the jobs as 'men's work' or 'women's work'. Although we have seen that pay *is* a real difference between men's and women's work, the explanations we have already listed might be the *reasons* for women getting low pay. Which do you think came first – the low pay or the kind of job? Let's look at our list of reasons again.

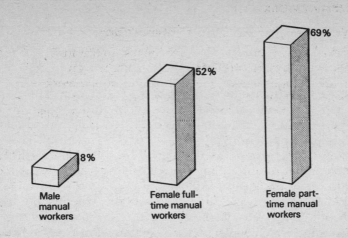

*Figure 1* Manual workers earning less than £1 per hour in 1975

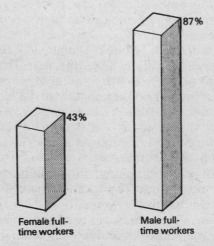

*Figure 2* Workers earning more than £60 per week in 1979

We say women wouldn't want to work on an oily machine – but are quite happy with the idea of women working in hospital laundries or picking potatoes. Different kinds of dirt maybe, but . . .

An interesting example of the way we think of 'skill' is the change this century in who does typewriting. When typewriters were first introduced and regarded as highly technical pieces of equipment, typing was a man's job, well-paid. Now typing is a woman's job, badly-paid, and typing as a *skill* is not regarded as anything particularly special. We will be returning to the idea of skill later.

We can perhaps get another idea about whether the type of work or the rate of pay comes first by looking at a few other jobs which have had a sex-change. In the world of computer technology, most of the research posts were held by women until around 1950, when men began to take over those jobs. The same thing happened in broadcasting; large numbers of women held quite key jobs in the early days, and few do so now. Both of these industries have expanded rapidly, and gone from being regarded as rather an odd line of work to being well paid and having quite a lot of status. Is that why those jobs changed sex? Why does any job change sex? And how do they come to be men's or women's work in the first place?

How do we decide what is women's – or men's work? Remember the fish-filleter from the list? This is a peculiar example, and unless you live in an area where fish-processing is a major industry, you probably had a bit of a job trying to decide which sex would be likely to do this job. But here's the funny thing. If you live around Hull or Grimsby you would think of hand-filleting as a man's job – practically every hand-filleter in the area is a man. If you live in the North-east of Scotland you will probably have said the job is women's work – around 70 per cent of hand-filleters in Aberdeen and Fraserburgh are women.

There doesn't seem to be an easy explanation. The job is unpleasant, wet and cold, and filleters often get arthritis and dermatitis. The kinds of fish landed in the two areas are different, but not so different that you could explain it by saying that the women in North East Scotland have to do finer work on smaller fish. Lots of the work in Aberdeen is done on a casual basis, but wage rates are about the same in the two areas. And yet people in Hull and Grimsby are convinced that hand-filleting is a man's job, and people in North East Scotland will tell you the same job is really women's work.

Another example comes from the textile industry. The introduction of the spinning mule at the time of the Industrial Revolution led to the employment of mule spinners – skilled workers, usually men. A further technical improvement in the early part of the nineteenth century produced the self-acting mule, a machine which did not require anything like the same level of skill from the operator. The self-acting mule was introduced in both the cotton mills of Lancashire and Glasgow. In both places unions fought to retain the skilled status of the work, but different solutions were reached. In Lancashire, the job remained skilled 'men's work'. In Glasgow, the job was transformed into women's work, 'skilled men' being employed as overlookers for a number of women, with the women operating the machines. So in the two places there was a difference not only between what work was regarded as skilled or unskilled, but also between what was regarded as 'men's work' and 'women's work'.

We still haven't got to the bottom of what makes us think of some jobs as men's work and others as women's work. There are a lot of puzzling inconsistencies in this area – and perhaps by now you may be thinking it doesn't matter. Now we have the Sex Discrimination Act, either sex can apply for any job anyway. But our ideas are still quite fixed. Don't you get a surprise when you see a man in a typing pool, or when you see a woman engineer? It's a very simple and obvious point, and one which we are all aware of if we think about the jobs people we know do: in general, men and women do different jobs.

Women do office work, provide services (professional, technical, clerical, domestic, catering, etc.) and work in the

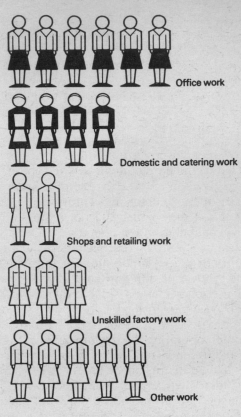

Office work

Domestic and catering work

Shops and retailing work

Unskilled factory work

Other work

Each figure represents 5% of all women in work

*Figure 3*   What sort of work do women do?

distributive trades (shops, warehouses and mail order). See Figure 3. These jobs accounted for 58 per cent of the women at work in 1978 – more than in 1966, when only 52 per cent of women at work, worked in these jobs. Men work in a much wider range of jobs and industries.

The question that immediately springs to mind is 'why do women and men end up in different jobs?' There are lots of possible explanations – let's list a few:

24

- tradition;
- certain jobs are more suitable either for women or for men;
- employers prefer women or men for particular kinds of work;
- women or men are the only ones prepared to work at certain jobs;
- women are prepared to work for lower wages than men;
- women are not interested in a career or promotion prospects;
- women don't really want skilled or responsible jobs because they know they will have to give up to have children;
- our education and training systems make boys and girls go into different jobs;
- women work in those jobs which fit in with domestic responsibilities.

Can you think of any other reasons? Which reasons do you think help to make sense of the situation? Do they make sense of the examples – typing, fish-filleting and spinning? Right through this book we will be looking at this problem of what makes women's work different from men's work, and the effects of this difference on trade union organization. Before we move on to look at these let's just go back over one point again. Remember that women who do paid work are mostly working in the service industries. And remember that the proportion of working women who work in the service industries is growing. In other words, women are still doing 'women's work', and even more of us are working at 'women's jobs' now than was the case ten years ago. In that ten years we have heard a lot about the Sex Discrimination Act. Why aren't women moving into some of the jobs we call 'men's work'? Let's think about why things are not changing at the same time as we think about the reasons men and women tend to do different jobs.

## 'Different but equal'

We have just listed some of the possible reasons why men and women end up in different jobs. Let's take up two of these ideas now:

● certain jobs are more suitable either for men or women;
● our education and training systems makes girls and boys go into different jobs.

It's getting less popular nowadays to say that women are inferior to men (though you must know someone who still says this!). But lots of people say that men and women are very different; so different that some jobs are obviously not suitable for men, and others are not appropriate for women. You must have heard the man who just about collapses if he has to run from the pub to catch the bus home telling his mates how women just wouldn't be strong enough to do *his* job – after all even now women athletes can't run as fast as men. Or the woman who says she wouldn't be able to lift heavy weights in her job – but is managing to carry a screaming toddler *and* three heavy bags of shopping!

But to be serious, do the differences between men and women matter a lot? In the Soviet Union, where all jobs used to be open to people of both sexes, a new list of one hundred jobs 'unsuitable' for women was published to take effect from January 1981. Were they right before, or are they right now? Are we right in this country in the way we think of women's and men's jobs? What are the differences between the natural talents of women and those of men – in fact, are there any differences at all?

Psychologists and child development specialists have spent years arguing about the differences between men's and women's intelligence, personality, ability to learn particular skills and so on. Some say there are no differences, some say that the differences between the sexes are inborn, some say that boys and girls learn to behave differently because they are treated differently from the moment that first crucial question is asked – 'Is it a boy or a girl?'

One of the common statements about the different abilities

of men and women is that men are more mechanically minded than women. Some researchers have gone so far as to suggest that this is because a certain part of the right-hand side of men's brains tends to be larger than the same bit in women – and that women's superior vocabulary and use of language relates to an area on the left of the brain which is bigger in women.

It's very tempting as a woman to laugh at this and not to think too hard about the effect reading about ideas like this has on people. Even if these ideas *are* true it doesn't automatically mean that the divisions between men's work and women's work don't need to be challenged. So we need to take two quite distinct steps to work out:

*First* what differences are there between men and women (in addition to the obvious ones!) and how do these differences come about?

*Second* once we know about the differences, what is the best way to make sure we use each person's special talents to the best effect?

This book is far too short to go into these questions in detail, but we can take a quick look at them. Perhaps a couple of examples will help to illustrate why we need to look at *both* the questions before we really get to the point.

Let's take the example of skill in the use of language. Most experts will tell you that girls learn to talk earlier and more fluently and, *on average*, are better than boys at writing, spelling and so on. If you had to decide how money should be spent on education for children – who should get the best teachers, equipment and so on – would you, based on the information that girls are better than boys at language, conclude that the money would best be put to use helping along the natural talents of girls? Or that special remedial help should be given to the boys?

Before we look at that question any further, let's take another example. Again, most experts agree that boys have a greater aptitude than girls for metalwork. Given that, should more time and money be spent on boys training in metalwork or on girls?

Have you chosen the same solution to both questions? Of course, what happens in practice is that both sexes probably get an equal chance at reading and writing and that boys still tend to get a better chance to do metalwork. (Research carried out in Scotland in 1980/81 indicates that, although boys are taking domestic science in some schools, girls are still being refused woodwork and other practical and technical subjects.)

Of course, it is possible to argue that being able to read and write is so important that both sexes must get an equal chance – and that metalwork is an important qualification for boys trying for apprenticeships. But this is obviously a circular argument; as long as boys rather than girls go for apprenticeships they will have more need of metalwork – and if girls try to get apprenticeships they won't have the right qualifications. So perhaps going for the remedial approach is better – and necessary if girls are ever to get jobs in the traditional male domains. This approach seems even more obvious when we look at language, if our educational system had refused boys the right to acquire skills in this area we would never have had the chance to read books by many famous male writers.

Perhaps all this is beginning to make clear what was wrong with the question we asked in the first place. If boys are better *on average* than girls at one skill, and girls are better *on average* than boys at another skill, this is no justification for concentrating attention on one or the other. Convenient as it may be to divide the world up into just two groups – male and female – by doing this we will be bound to waste individual talents by refusing to look at what each individual is good at, concentrating instead on what their particular sex happens to be better at *on average*.

One more example may make this clearer. Imagine that several psychologists have been studying the special skills of first-born children, and have discovered that they tend to be much better at sciences than their younger brothers and sisters. The psychologists publish their results, and the government decides that in view of the greater talents of first-born children, all secondary schools will offer special science courses for first-born children. Other children will not be given many science lessons – just enough to teach them a little about the subject. Jobs and courses in science will of course still require applicants to hold a qualification in science.

A scheme like this would cause a public outcry. Parents would demand that their talented younger children should get a chance to do science, and that first-born children who are no good at science should get the chance to do something else instead. And yet if you go through this ludicrous example sustituting 'boys' for 'first-born', and 'girls' for 'other children' and 'metalwork' for 'science' this is what happened everywhere until fifteen years ago – and still happens in many cases. And parents still put up with it.

Access to training, then, may well depend on school courses. If school courses lump all boys and all girls together talented individuals may lose out, missing the chance to get on a training course or apprenticeship.

But the whole thing goes much deeper than subjects offered at school. By the time girls get to secondary school, very few are keen enough on metalwork to *want* to learn about it and very few boys are going to be thinking of a career as a secretary.

What has happened to these children? Were girls born wanting to be typists, or boys born wanting to learn a trade? Or if that's taking things too far, were girls born feminine and boys born manly? Lots of people have been trying to find an answer to these questions in the last few years, and one thing is coming out quite clearly: from the earliest days of a baby's life, adults respond to the child differently depending on whether they think it is a boy or girl. One researcher showed this by hoodwinking adults into thinking boy toddlers were girls and vice versa, as well as watching people dealing with real girls and real boys. The adults reacted one way to children they believed were girls, whether or not they actually *were* girls, and another way to the 'boy' toddlers.

Adults apparently encourage passive and sociable behav-

29

iour in girls and active and independent behaviour in boys. Add to this the fact that as soon as children begin to take notice of the way people around them behave they will notice that men and women behave differently and spend their time in different ways and that boys and girls seem to have different lifestyles, too. A picture will begin to build up. At school they will probably choose the same subjects as their friends – who will usually be of the same sex. Put on top of that the fact that boys are encourged to learn about mechanical things, and you begin to understand why even a girl who *has* deliberately chosen metalwork at school and gone on to an engineering apprenticeship can say this:

At Tech, when we were doing properties of materials, the lecturer would bring along a part of a car and say 'That's why it's made of this metal, this material.' The lads would know what it was on a car and what it did. We had to ask 'Well, what is it then?'

So perhaps this is part of the story. Girls and boys are treated differently from early childhood, both at home and at school, and end up with different skills. But there's another side to this question too. More and more if you talk to women and girls they will look at a list of jobs like the one we looked at earlier in the chapter and say, 'Of course, men or women can really do any of these jobs nowadays.' But if you ask, 'What job will you be doing as your next job?' most women and girls will still answer with a job that does fit the idea of 'women's work'. We have all heard about equal opportunities, and we are all used to seeing the adverts for 'Foreman/woman', 'Barman/barmaid' and so on. But most people still don't really think about *themselves* applying for a job that is usually done by the opposite sex. We all tend to think some *other* woman will be able to apply for the job as 'Draughtsman/woman' or perhaps that some *other* man will apply for the job as 'Personal secretary (male/female)'. It takes a bit more time to persuade ourselves we could actually do these jobs.

One of the most interesting insights into what women and men expect of jobs comes from this example of a well-paid professional job.

An employer was looking for someone to do quite a high-powered job. The job was advertised at a salary of £10,000 a year, and when the applications came in, only a very few women had applied, although the employer knew there were lots of well-qualified women around who could do the job. The advert was changed, and this time heaps of applications came in from women and very few from men. The change in the advert was simple – nothing had been altered except the salary, which appeared the second time as £5,000 a year.

The idea that women get paid badly is obviously so well-learnt by each of us that many women don't even bother to apply for a well-paid job. Do you think this example could give us a clue as to why women don't generally apply for men's jobs? Is it that we don't think an employer will be prepared to pay a reasonable wage for a woman? Perhaps women are also afraid that jobs may be too heavy or too dirty. Ginny, a carpenter and joiner with a local council in England, has this to say:

'When it comes to lifting, I'm as strong as the male apprentices. I can lift what they can. The older blokes who have been using their bodies as a means of earning a living for ten, fifteen, twenty-five years, naturally they're stronger. But a lot of it's a question of technique, knowing just when and how to lift things. I did push myself when I started. I wanted to try everything, so I did some astonishing things, but now I'm more inclined to just ask someone to help me because that's what the men do. It doesn't make me feel weak and feeble. It's a matter of common sense. If something's too heavy for one person, two people carry it.'

Ginny has now gained enough confidence not to mind asking for help. How many women would never try this kind of job *in case* they turned out to be weak and people laughed at them?

There are also other factors. Lots of women – quite reasonably – don't fancy working as the only woman in a place full of men, and most men – joking apart – probably feel the same about being the only man. We are all guilty of often not working out what we *really* want to do, but simply taking the first job that comes along; of course with the unemployment figures rising, that's a very sensible thing to do. In fact, rising unemployment and economic recession are much more effective at keeping women in the traditional 'women's jobs' than any law could be in helping them escape from badly paid 'women's work'.

Most people are probably a bit shy of drawing attention to themselves and one thing you can be sure of is that if you take a job that's usually done by someone of the opposite sex, you will get a lot of attention. How many times have you asked a bus driver why he became a bus driver? Ask Katrina, the bus driver in Aberdeen, how many times each day she has to answer that question from a passenger and you'll get a different reply. She'll also tell you how many people ask if it isn't awfully heavy work (imagine asking a man!) and her fund of jokes about women drivers must include just about every one there is. Would most people be prepared to put up with this – or would they prefer a quiet life?

## Don't men and women have different skills?

There is one other thing to look at when we are talking about whether men or women are more suited to particular jobs. Lots of 'men's jobs' are regarded as skilled, the fight for skilled status has always been an important one for trade unions. Skilled status has always carried benefits, particularly if the skill is scarce – people will find it easy to get a job if they have a skill which not many others have, and which is needed in industry. Of course, having a skill never guaranteed anyone a job, but it does help. If you have a skill you will generally be better paid than unskilled workers. If your employer needs your skill, and doesn't want you to leave your job – perhaps because she or he is not sure you can be replaced – that puts you in a good position to go further than asking for better pay. You can start to make demands for better conditions, better hours, and more control over how you organize your own work – and the employer may decide to give way rather than risk losing a skilled worker.

Trade unions have, from the early days, recognized the

greater bargaining power of the skilled worker as opposed to the unskilled worker, who can be much more easily replaced, except at times when labour is very scarce. Of course, skilled workers lose this advantage if the particular skill is held by many people, all competing for the few jobs which use that skill. So the early craft unions – unions of skilled workers – saw how important it was that they had control over the number of people learning a skill, and fought hard to influence the number of apprentices trained and the standards of training provided.

But we have left out an important question. What do we mean when we talk about a 'skill', or about a particular job being 'skilled' or 'unskilled'? Sometimes it's a bit difficult to see what we *do* mean, especially when we look at some of the men's jobs which are regarded as skilled, and some of the jobs women do which we think of as unskilled. Is a skill something which involves manual dexterity – an ability to use our hands to do certain tasks? Is a skill any practical ability which requires thought or knowledge? Or is a skill the ability to carry out a wide range of related tasks rather than one particular operation? Or is it anything you have to do an apprenticeship for? Let's look at some examples.

Do you remember the example of 'men's work' and 'women's work' from the textile industry? When the self-acting mule was introduced for spinning the unions fought to retain skilled status although the job itself had been made less skilled by the new machinery. In various industries union insistence on the holding of a union card combined with insistence that cards only be issued to those who have completed a course of training managed to keep skilled status for jobs which would otherwise have been given a new description, as semi-skilled or unskilled.

The point of all this is that it's not necessarily just the length of training required for a job which has defined that job as skilled or not. It has often been in the employers' interests to define jobs as semi-skilled or unskilled – and in union interests to define the same jobs as skilled. The label that eventually gets stuck on a job can be as much a reflection of the balance of power between union and employer as it is of the length of time taken to learn the job. So well-organized unions have been able to fight to keep craft status for their members' jobs, whereas weak or badly organized unions have had to concede that their members' jobs are semi- or unskilled.

What is all this to do with 'women's work'? Let's look back at the points we have collected so far:

● Skills can give a worker more bargaining power; either because her or his skills are in short supply, or because she or he has such a wide range of skills that finding another job would be easy – there is no need to stay in a particular factory making one kind of product, the skilled worker can go wherever the best opportunities are. The worker who has learnt to do one operation on one product doesn't have this choice.

● When a skill is downgraded by improved machinery, some unions have been able to fight to keep skilled status by using union muscle, even though the job no longer requires as much skill.

● Skilled workers (or workers doing jobs still labelled as skilled, entry to which is controlled by the union) can fight better for improved pay and conditions.

● Women manual workers earn a lot less than men per hour, and often have worse conditions.

Is there any link between these statements?

**Length of training**  Statistics on women at work show that the jobs women manual workers do are mostly described as unskilled or semi-skilled – far more male manual workers do jobs which are regarded as skilled – a craft or 'a trade'. Statistics also show that this century the proportion of women with a skill is dropping – at the same time as a larger and larger proportion of men are being trained for skilled jobs.

But we saw earlier that the idea of a skill can depend on two things:

● The actual time taken to learn the job – usually a wide range of different tasks. (For example, a skilled engineering worker will be able to operate a lot of different machines and processes and make or do several different things with each machine or process.)

 The extent to which the union has been able to fight for or keep skilled status.

For which of these reasons do you think women's jobs are often described as semi-skilled or unskilled? Or do both reasons have something to do with it? Let's look at the training itself first. A report by Nancy Seear in 1971 said:

'The need to make better use of manpower (yes, she did say *man-power*!) is constantly stressed. Yet the position is tolerated, as in the UK, where about three quarters of all women in employment are in jobs which take less than six months to learn.'

So most women *are* doing jobs which can be learnt quite quickly – or, to be accurate, only need at most six months extra training to learn. (Could you teach anyone to do the full range of a cleaner's job in six months if they had never seen anyone doing any cleaning before, let alone practised for years in their own home? Maybe, but . . . ) Another survey in the late sixties, done by Audrey Hunt, found that one in five women workers then had a training or a qualification which was not needed for the job they were doing: most of them were women who had found it difficult to return to the work they had done before bringing up a family. So, to sum up, three quarters of women workers do jobs which only need a short training. And quite a few of these women had originally been trained for better jobs, but found it difficult to return to them later.

**Union demands for recognition of skills**  What about the other possibility, union pressure to define jobs as skilled or semi-skilled? Have you ever heard of a clerical worker say anything like this?

'Everyone seems to think I was born sitting at a typewriter and knowing what to do, just because I'm a woman. I had to learn to type, just like anyone learns a skill, and if I get out of practice I lose my speed and accuracy – just like anyone else with a skill does.'

Typists do in fact have to have a wide range of skills – you will know this if you are a typist yourself, if not ask someone who is. Lots of girls start learning to type at school, go on to take college courses, and usually have to clock up quite a bit of experience before anyone will take them on as anything but the office junior. Have you ever seen a union pressing for better wages for typists on the grounds that they should get parity – equality of pay and conditions – with shop-floor workers who have spent a similar length of time in training? (It has been done, by the way, but it is not the line that unions usually take.) Parity on these terms would drastically improve many clerical workers' conditions – an issue we will take up again when we talk about equal pay.

Could a union make a case for giving a home help skilled status? Make a list of the arguments that could be put forward to show that a home help's job is skilled – and for comparison note down qualities required by a skilled job you know about – perhaps that of a joiner or an engineer.

Now look at this list:

- Safe and efficient use of hand- and power-tools.
- Correct use of chemicals.
- Ability to identify and carry out necessary operations given general instructions.

Which job does that list apply to? A joiner and an engineer both use power-tools – electric drills, lathes, milling machines power-saws and so on all fall into that group; and they also both use hand-tools – chisels, hammers and a variety of others. They both work with chemicals – glues perhaps, or degreasing fluids, and they are both expected to understand instructions like 'we need twenty parts like those shown in this drawing' or 'renew all the window frames'. Both the joiner and the engineer would have to decide what tools to use, what needs to be done first, and the most efficient way to do the job. Clearly skilled jobs, wouldn't you think?

Now let's look at the home help. She (you don't catch many men doing this job) may work with various power-tools (vacuum cleaners, washing-machines, electric floor-polishers) and will certainly use a wide range of hand-tools (brooms, dusters, scourers). She works with a lot of chemicals – some pretty safe, like detergents and polishes, other more hazardous, like bleaches and disinfectants. If she is given an instruction like 'Go to Mrs Smith's on Tuesday mornings' she is expected to be able to decide what tools and what chemicals to use in a wide variety of situations and to be able to plan the most efficient order in which to do the various tasks necessary. For example, it doesn't do much good to clean a carpet before cleaning soot and ash from an open fire – or to use bleach and a hoover to polish a table.

Is this a ridiculous comparison to draw between the jobs? Why does it seem ridiculous? Is it because a skill that a lot of women have is not very highly regarded because they employ it *unpaid* in their own homes? (This all comes back to the idea that a *real* skill is worth good wages.) About one out of every five women who go out to work do work which can be described as 'domestic and catering' work. Many of these jobs are regarded as unskilled, or at best semi-skilled. Does the example of the home help make you question these definitions?

If this example has still left you unconvinced that domestic work is skilled, you are not alone. Most people have that point of view – and most unions have traditionally agreed with them. But if we really want to look carefully at women's work the issue of skill is an important one, and it's important for us as trade unionists to sort out what we think about skills. We must decide:

● If the skills women use at work are being given proper recognition.
● If we have the trade union strength to be able to fight for the improved pay and conditions that go with skilled status.

What do you think?

## What future is there for skilled work anyway?

Something may have struck you while we've been talking about skills. We hear a lot about the silicon chip and new technology. We have got used to the idea of cars built by robots, we have heard about new printing techniques, using computers, which could revolutionize the newspaper industry (you may even work with these machines) and more and more people seem to be casually dropping words like 'visual display unit (VDU)' or 'word processor' into conversations. Trade unions have been confronted by technological changes before; at the time of the Industrial Revolution, when cheap machinery that could be used in the worker's own home began to be superceded by more efficient, expensive machines which only factory owners could afford; and during the 1950s, when the key word was 'automation'. These are two of the more famous examples – both involved a loss of jobs for workers on the old processes, and eventually new jobs on the newer processes. The key trade union issues were, and still are, what happens to the workers whose jobs are lost, and what effect will the new processes have on workers' conditions.

The difference with the new technology of the 1980s is that for the first time, the majority of jobs at risk are women's jobs, especially office jobs. Fans of new technology will tell you that, for example, being a word processor operator is much more interesting than working in a typing pool, typing hundreds of identical standard letters. But this needn't necessarily be the case. Employers are not suddenly going to start dreaming up more interesting jobs for workers – or are they? An employer will be most interested in increasing the amount of work done, or in improving efficiency. New technology could eliminate boring, routine, work – but will it? There is no reason why employers will change the view they have of women's work, as this example shows. One manufacturer is already promoting computerized office equipment by describing the work 'your secretary' can get through on the new keyboard linked to a computer (standard letters, reports, minutes and so on) and then saying that the company's finance expert will be able to use another part of the same keyboard for his (yes, his!) calculations while 'your girl is doing the post'. Nothing has changed – the woman is still doing the typing, inches away from more keys that could make her job much more interesting. And the man is still taking home the higher wage for the high status job.

Unions will need to do some hard thinking to come up with the right approach to new technology and the skills it will require from workers. Meantime, we could do worse than aiming for ample retraining opportunities for all workers, avoiding the situation where a very few jobs are skilled, and the rest are routine and boring (and probably done by low-paid women), and making sure that flexible working hours are to the worker's advantage, not just management's.

The very nature of skills is changing under pressure from developments in technology. The way the unions respond now will be crucial to the way we will be describing skilled work in twenty years' time – and to the number of people who are still in work then. How that situation works out will also depend on the training opportunities we are giving to girls and boys now.

## Why do girls and boys learn different skills?

There's another question we haven't looked at about skills. Why do girls and boys learn different skills? Practically all the girls who do apprenticeships do them in hairdressing. Why don't they go for training which would get them a better paid job?

There seem to be two main reasons why girls don't try to learn 'men's' skills. A girl may well be the one and only girl on a course – it takes a real brass neck to make yourself a centre of attraction and its pretty difficult to blend in with the surroundings if you're the only female present. The other relates to the way the different sexes are treated, even as small children. Girls don't play as much as boys at using the 'male' skills, and there are still more parents who would be horrified if their daughter couldn't sew on a button than would complain that she couldn't wire up an electric plug. Sandy, a woman electrician has managed to get over both these problems – how many girls do you think would do the same?

'Handling tools is new to some girls, but I used to help me Dad do things so I was fairly used to it. You do get a few stares when you go into a caff full of blokes for your lunch-break, wearing overalls and with dirty hands, but you soon get used to that.'

More women are going into retraining on the government's Training Opportunities Scheme (TOPS) courses in the traditionally male areas. But quite a few have come to grief and had to leave or change courses as a result of poor skills with tools. TOPS courses mostly demand reasonable English and Maths, and set tests on these subjects, but applicants for most courses are told they don't need prior knowledge of metalwork, woodwork or other skills. Most women who finished school before 1975 didn't get the chance to learn these skills at school – and most weren't like Sandy, the electrician who helped her dad.

Men who go to TOPS courses for craft skills will usually be people who have done a metalwork or woodwork course at school, and who will, in any case, probably have been encouraged by family and friends to learn to use and practise using hammers, chisels, files and so on. Women without this background may seem very slow to grasp more specialized craft skills. What would you do to improve their chances? One good scheme took girls through a special course – like a remedial course really – to learn how to use tools and acquire some of the basic skills most boys have picked up somewhere along the line. These girls showed a much greater success rate in their later apprenticeships than girls usually do. Perhaps one of the key features of this scheme was that the girls did go on to conventional apprenticeships. One major disadvantage of the TOPS courses is that, unlike most skills training in this country, people are given a students' allowance to study full-time, rather than wages paid by their employer on a day release basis. This means there is no ready-made employer at the end of the course – which doesn't help TOPS trainees to get a job. Should we be negotiating with employers to provide pre-apprenticeship training schemes for girls? Or would it be better to follow the example of some European countries and take this type of training out of the hands of the employers by providing state-funded full-time courses for everyone *before* they get a job? Think about the advantages and disadvantages, both from the point of view of all workers, and from the point of view of encouraging women to learn the traditional male skills. What kind of training would you want to see?

## Why do men and women do different jobs?

This section started out by asking why men and women end up in different jobs, and whether there is any point in looking for change through education and training. It's up to you to decide if you think trade unions should start to think in a new way about skills, and if so what the unions should do. But let's give the last word on this for now to Ginny, the carpenter and joiner who talked about physical strength earlier on – she has a pretty positive attitude to women going into her line of work.

'The money's good, especially for girls. And I think its exciting to be part of building the environment. I mean, when you walk down the street, every single thing you see has been put up by men. That's quite amazing, that women had no part in the construction of the whole planet practically. It's time we took part. It's really exciting.'

Now you have read this chapter, you should have some idea what sort of work women do, and how different it is from the work men do. Have you begun to wonder about why things are as they are, or about whether there is anything which ought to be changed about the jobs women and men do and the skills they use? These question set the scene for the rest of the book, and should help us to understand more about the way women do or don't fit into the trade union movement. In the next chapter, though, we will be filling in a bit more of the background, and looking at the other job most women have – caring for a home and, perhaps, a family.

# Further reading

The Gender Trap Book 1: Education and work Carol Adams and Rae Laurikietus (Virago, 1980). Although this book is written mostly for use in schools and colleges it is probably the best introduction to the things we have looked at in this chapter. Beware, though, the description of what the Sex Discrimination Act says is incorrect.

*Women at Work* Lindsay Mackie and Polly Pattullo (Tavistock, 1977). This book is a lot more detailed, and contains a lot of relevant facts and figures, along with interesting examples from real life.

*Womens Work, Mens Work – the Ambivalence of Equality* Virginia Novarra (Marion Boyars Publishers Ltd, 1980). Have you ever thought it's really the secretaries who do the work in business? Or that women's work in the home is harder than going to business lunches? If so, you will like this book, even though it is written more from the point of view of a professional woman – not the most typical woman worker. It's very readable, but you will have to be prepared to think quite hard.

*Equality for some* Jane Thompson (National Extension College, 1980). This handbook, and the tape recordings which go with it, looks at the whole range of problems facing women at work.

Women and Manual Trades are a group of women who produce a newsletter and have compiled a report on TOPS courses. Contact them via Women and Manual Trades, First of May Bookshop, 43 Candlemaker Row, Edinburgh.

The largest collection of British songs about women is *My Song is my Own*, edited by Kathy Henderson with Frankie Armstrong and Sandra Kerr (Pluto Press, 1979). Lots of the songs put questions about women's lives and work into a sharper form than you will see anywhere else.

# Chapter **Two**

## Two jobs – the twenty-four-hour day

We have seen that men and women do different kinds of jobs and learn different skills, but we haven't yet looked at the other job that most women do – housework. In this chapter we will be looking at the position of a worker who also has to do housework, and perhaps look after children too. By the end of this chaper we will have looked at the following questions:

● Are women housewives first, workers second; and if so, what effect does this have? Who benefits from women being regarded as housewives?

● What effects do pensions, tax, benefits and social services have in keeping men out at work and women working in the home?
● What happens to workers who have children? Are the needs of parents taken into account by employers, trade unions, and the government?
● Is the right to the choice to have children or not anything to do with trade unions?

## Housewives first, workers second?

If someone says to you 'A woman's work . . .' you would probably finish off the sentence with either '. . . is in the home' or ' . . .is never done'. Either way, it's pretty clear the woman we are talking about is a housewife – probably a mother too. Most women who go out to work have an unpaid job at home as well – and this unpaid job affects lots of aspects of our paid work. Let's list a few.

**Hours** Many women work part-time (about 40 per cent of all women workers) and many full-timers also have to choose their working hours carefully to fit in with domestic responsibilities, especially childcare.

**Rates of pay** The idea that paid work is a second job for a housewife is one of the things that keeps pay low – an employer prepared to offer part-time work often expects not to have to pay as much. A particularly bad example of this is homework, mostly done by women who actually have no choice but to try and earn money *at home* because they cannot leave their dependants – children, disabled people, or elderly relatives – unattended. In a small survey done by the Low Pay Unit in 1979, half of the workers earned less than 40p an hour for knitting, packing cards and envelopes, machine sewing and so on. For these women, who are forced to make domestic responsibilities a priority, pay is at its worst.

**Choice of jobs** Most families live where the main breadwinner's job is. In five out of six families this is a man. So in most families, women have to find jobs near where the family already lives – this may well restrict the choice of jobs and also the opportunities for promotion, which often involves a move or an absence from home for training.

**Training and education**  As we saw in the last chapter, far less girls than boys learn a skill or take a long course of study for a job. One of the reasons may well be the 'You'll just get married anyway' attitude which can come from teachers, parents, friends or employers. A girl can always be sure of a job as a housewife.

**Job security**  A lot of people still say 'the married women should go first' when they hear about redundancies. Even though selecting only married women for redundancy would be illegal, it's quite legal to pay off all the part-timers which often comes to more or less the same thing.

But is the idea that women's real work is housework and childcare still believed by many people? Let's look at a few things you might overhear in the bus or the pub or in a supermarket queue:

'Of course, all these working mothers can't keep a proper eye on their teenagers.'
'I often help my wife with the housework.'
'Our kids have always been brought up to help in the house – we're not there to wait on them.'
'I always like to be at home when the boys get back from school.'
'I wish I could earn enough that my wife didn't have to go out to work.'
'I don't really feel I should go back to work until the girls are both settled in at school.'
'It really makes me mad that some people seem to think I'm a bad mother because I go out to work. It's *for* the children I go out to work, so we can have a reasonable standard of living.'
'Even though we both work full-time, and he does do a fair bit at home, I still feel the housework ends up as my responsibility and he thinks he's doing me a favour.'
'I don't know what I would do without my mum. I couldn't manage

45

if she didn't help out when the kids are ill or on their school holidays.'

Who would you expect to have said each of those things? Someone older or younger, a man or woman? Which things might you say yourself?

We don't all have the same ideas about women's responsibilities in the home, though it's obvious that our ideas are changing. Most families now depend on a woman's wage in one way or another – surveys show that the number of families who would be able to claim Family Income Supplement to make up their low wages to a more reasonable level would increase dramatically if it were not for a woman's wage helping to make ends meet. About half of all married women go out to work. A quarter of women with at least one child under four go out to work. Three quarters of women with children over ten go out to work. Something has to give at home – men are doing more. But you must have seen articles in the papers about surveys on who actually does most of the housework – it's still women, even if they go out to work full time. It's also quite enlightening to read some of the sums insurance companies have done on what it really costs to replace a wife with paid workers – cleaners, cooks, counsellors, children's nurses, teachers, nurses, administrators, personal secretaries and so on. Even back in 1975 the Legal & General Insurance Company estimated that replacing a mother's services with nanny, housekeeper and cleaning lady would cost at least £71 a week.

Women's work in the home makes it possible for a lot of men to go out and work. A song by Sandra Kerr called 'The Maintenance Engineer' which describes a housewife's work as maintenance puts this especially well:

'The truth began to dawn then how I keep him fit and trim,
So the boss can make a nice fat profit out of me and him
And as a solid union man he got in quite a rage
To think that we're both working hard and getting one man's wage
I said 'And what about the part-time packing job I do –
That's three men that I work for, love – my boss, your boss, and you.'

Do you think housework is given enough value? How would you like to see things change, if at all? Does housework *have* to be done in our homes? Should we try to shift around who does the housework *within* the family or should we try to get rid of as much housework as possible by encouraging the growth of public and community services? (It's worth thinking for a moment about the way public spending cuts throw more work at the housewife by reducing services – school meals, old people's homes, care of the chronic sick and disabled.)

But we started out looking at housework because of the way people who have to do the housework still have to fit it in when they do a paid job. The idea that all women are housewives first, and paid workers second has a lot to answer for. It crops up throughout history and in lots of different societies – and it usually ends up as an excuse for treating women worse then men. (A third of all women workers are not married but they too suffer from the general assumption that all women are really dependent on a male breadwinner's wage.)

The same idea is a good excuse for kicking women out of the labour market when paid work is scarce (the women should be at home anyway). But it still lets employers call them back to work when there is a labour shortage.

The same excuse comes in handy again when setting women's wage rates – as work outside the home is not a woman's *real* job, she obviously doesn't need good wages; and in any case she won't be as good a worker as a man as *her* special skills are in domestic work.

Employers are not the only ones who find the idea that women's work is in the home comes in handy. Some large trade unions, until only forty years ago, excluded women from membership altogether – other unions continued to exclude women until the Sex Discrimination Act required them to 'pair up' with unions which catered solely for women in similar jobs. The reasons the unions gave were the same old excuses in another form:

● Women aren't permanently on the labour market – they

47

can at any time return to unpaid work at home and therefore can't be relied upon to support long-term trade union struggles to improve conditions.
● Women don't need, and certainly aren't prepared to fight for, better wages.

## Who benefits?

If employers and unions seem to be using the same excuses, we need to work out who really stands to gain from people accepting these excuses. Some people would argue it's a male conspiracy to keep women running about looking after men, and making sure men get the best deal at work. The argument goes that men benefit because:

● They get looked after at home, and manage to get out of doing all their share of caring for their children.
● Without competition from women at work men get first pick of the best jobs and a better chance to learn a skill.
● After getting pushed around at work all day, at least they can be boss in their own homes – after all, they are the breadwinner.
● They may be cushioned from redundancy by encouraging women workers back to the home when jobs are scarce.
● As a result of better training opportunities and the skilled worker status we looked at in Chapter one, union organization is stronger and wages and conditions are better.

Other people argue that it's employers who benefit, because:

● They get plenty of extra people to call on when production demands more workers – without having to pay to keep them around when there's no work for them.
● They get a good excuse for not paying the rate for the job – it's only pin money anyway.
● The high labour turnover, with fluctuating demand makes women workers hard to organize into trade unions.
● Worse working conditions and lack of benefits like sick pay are better tolerated by part-time and temporary workers.

● By putting women into specific short-term jobs the women only need training for that job, rather than full training.

Where do the unions stand in this? Do they benefit or lose out? They might benefit by:

● Concentrating on organizing men and relying on the greater bargaining power resulting from demand for their skills to build a strong union.

● Organizing to exclude women from paid work and using this to bargain more effectively for men, demanding better wages – (to keep a family) and providing more secure and steady employment for male union members by preventing the employer taking on cheap labour.

But this kind of strength is not built on a very firm basis – unions could lose out at any time cheap non-union labour is available to employers and the union does not respond effectively. An alternative strategy is for unions to try to recruit anyone who might otherwise become cheap labour and take existing members' jobs; once this kind of organization is built, the union has a much more permanent source of strength. We will be returning to these strategies in the chapter on trade union organization.

So the idea that a woman's *real* job is in the home benefits men in some ways and employers in plenty of ways. Trade unions may be more successful in the short term because of this idea, but constantly face a threat of employers using cheap labour if they do not get women organized. The one group that clearly doesn't benefit is women – except those few who can genuinely afford not to do paid work and to either get paid help with the housework or afford to pay for labour-saving devices and services like restaurant meals. (Mind you, their men are usually getting a pretty good deal too!)

We skipped a bit quickly over the public services, though we did mention that better or worse public services can decrease or increase the amount of housework there is to do. A lack of public services hits women very hard. We can be left with the responsibilities of caring for the young, the sick and the old. Is it right that individuals should be responsible, rather than society as a whole taking responsibility? All of us have to be cared for at some time in our lives and if no one was prepared to care for babies – or have them, for that matter – we would soon find there were no workers to keep our industries and services going.

## The family and the welfare state

Social responsibilities versus family responsibilities is a big question. But the tax system, benefit system, social services and pensions depend on the idea of the family – perhaps more than you think. Income tax is based on taxing family units, the extra allowances for married men and for female dependants caring for the infirm betray an underlying philosophy that women's work is in the home and men are the main breadwinners – an idea which shows up again with the responsibility for paying income tax – which is the man's. A women's magazine got a major campaign going in the late seventies to protest against tax office practices – including the refusal to actually write to married women about their tax – the women's letters were replied to in letters to their husbands. The Equal Opportunities Commission have put a lot of the complaints together in a free booklet called 'Women and Income Tax', which also explains in quite a lot of detail the way the whole system of taxation treats women.

If you think the tax system relies too heavily on the conventional idea of the family as a male breadwinner and dependent wife and possibly other old, young, or female dependants, have a look at the social security system. It's the man who has to register for work if the family is to get unemployment benefit or social security – and when he registers he gets extra benefit for his 'dependants' including a working wife. If a married woman, or a woman living with a man, registers for work she may be entitled to unemployment benefit, but will get a lower rate if she's married and either way won't get any extra for the man. If she was only entitled to social security she would get nothing at all – it's up to the man to register and claim for her – and for her children, even if he is not their father. Family Income Supplement, the allowance payable to families with low incomes, can only be paid to families where the man is working, or where the woman is a single parent. A household supported by a woman's wage where the man is, for example, chronically sick or a student, cannot claim FIS the same household with the same income earned by a man with a chronically sick wife or a student wife *would* be entitled to claim.

The social services too have their own peculiarities. Men who are single parents are encouraged to go out and find a job rather than staying at home looking after children – and in some areas they may qualify for a home help too. Imagine a woman single parent being offered a home help! She is much more likely to be encouraged to stay at home and be a 'proper mother'.

Pensions are another problem area. Most schemes provide widow's pensions – far fewer provide widowers' pensions. Think of the effect this will have on a family who are considering swapping around the usual roles. If the man stays at home or takes just part-time work in order to take on a greater share of domestic responsibilities, the woman may find it quite hard to provide a financially secure future for the family. Giving up pension entitlements is quite a big step for any family, and it's not just pension schemes operated by insurance companies which work this way – the state system too works out in most cases giving better benefits to families where the main breadwinner has been a man, not a woman.

These are just brief examples, but they show that plenty of areas administered by central and local government still haven't caught up with the Sex Discrimination Act. (Just in case all this is beginning to make you want to complain, you can forget using the law. The Sex Discrimination Act is quite clear about all this – tax and the national insurance and social security systems are not covered by the Act – and pension schemes can legally offer quite different benefits to men and women as long as the scheme is open to both.)

# A fair deal for mothers?

Things get more complicated for most housewives when they are mothers too. Paid work and being a parent add up to a pretty big job – not just for women, of course, but also for men who are responsible for housework and childcare as well as going out to work. In the next part of this chapter we will be looking at the way people try to fit pregnancy and childcare into their working lives.

Let's start with pregnancy and then work through to the responsibilities of parents with teenage children. A whole range of problems face the pregnant worker.

**Her health and the health of the baby**   Will she be able to get time to attend ante-natal clinics? Will her work be more hazardous to her health, or to the baby's health? Will she be able to afford to take enough time off work to give herself a reasonable chance of getting enough rest?

Health must be a priority. One of the few things which trade unionists have welcomed in the 1980 Employment Act has been the right for women to take time off work for ante-natal care. Problems at birth for mothers and babies are much more common in working class families. Research has shown that these problems mostly relate to worse living standards and poverty, but ante-natal care can help to save lives and prevent handicap in the baby, so the right to get ante-natal care is a fundamental one.

Pregnant women are exposed to risks at work just like any other worker and these risks may be much more serious during pregnancy. Changes in the hormone levels in the blood during pregnancy or when taking the Pill make women more vulnerable to poisoning by many chemicals commonly used at work. Certain chemicals are also extremely dangerous to the developing child, even at much lower levels than those which present a hazard for adults. The unborn child can also be damaged by x-rays and some other kinds of radiation. Trade unions have a responsibility to act to protect the health of menbers and their future children. Read more about this in *Health and Safety at Work* – another book in this series.

Getting enough time to rest as well as doing paid work and housework – women's two jobs – can be a real problem for pregnant women and new mothers. Options which make part-time work or reduced hours a possibility for these women could be written into agreements between unions and employers.

**Financial security**  Will she be able to survive financially if she gives up work during late pregnancy and the first weeks of her baby's life? Can she afford to lose overtime or go on to part-time work or lose bonus if her health makes her unable to work long hours or work as fast? Financial security will only be provided for every woman when a right to paid maternity leave lasting at least twelve to eighteen weeks is established for all women at work. This would still compare pretty badly with most other European countries – you will probably expect Sweden to allow nine or ten months paid leave to either parent, but would you have guessed that in Austria mothers are entitled to a year's leave? Our legal minimum paid leave of six weeks at near to full pay – less if you don't get the National Insurance maternity allowance for any reason – makes Britain seem a bit on the mean side. Our rights here have strings attached too. You must have already put in at least two years continuous service with your employer by eleven weeks before your baby is due, *and* you must work at least sixteen hours a week, or have five years clocked up at eight hours or more a week. Unless trade unions negotiate better rights, women workers will remain very vulnerable financially – and any health difficulties in pregnancy which result in loss of wages will make matters worse – perhaps unions should negotiate agreements on this too?

**Job security**  Will she be sacked during pregnancy? Will she be able to return to her job if she takes time off to have a baby?

Job security is probably the most important of all. Up until a few years ago most women resigned themselves to the fact that they would probably lose their jobs if they got pregnant.

Recent years have seen improvements in both law (originally in the Employment Protection Act 1975) and in agreements negotiated by trade unions with employers. The law in 1975 give three main rights:

● Pregnancy became an 'inadmissible' reason for dismissal (in other words you could not be sacked for a reason to do with your pregnancy except in a few very special circumstances.)

● A small amount of maternity pay was guaranteed in some cases.

● Women's right to return to their jobs was established in some cases.

In 1980, with the Employment Act, we have seen a step back in the legal position, which makes it even more necessary that trade unionists improve things for their members by negotiating better collective agreements.

The Employment Protection Act 1975 originally gave a most important right to those women who qualified for the right to return to *their own* job up to twenty-nine weeks after the birth of their child. The 1980 Act has reduced this to a right to return to a suitable alternative job, and taken the right away altogether from women who work for employers who have five or less employees. This is a most crucial change, not just for the many women who lose the right altogether because they work for a small employer, but also for women in bigger undertakings. The right to return to your own job, in your old department and with your old workmates is quite different from being given a new job with a bunch of strangers, and perhaps at a different rate of pay or slightly different hours. (Hours will of course be very important if you are trying to fix up childcare for your new baby.)

You may hear people saying it's only fair to let employers have a bit of flexibility – it's a big job to move people around again so that a returning worker gets her own job back. But what would you expect when someone returns from sick leave? Or after recovering from an accident at work? If an executive has a heart attack and a long absence from work she or he is unlikely to be asked to do an equivalent job running another department. Why shouldn't mothers expect the same deal? After all, if no one has babies industry won't be able to run – women (and the few men) who give up working time to look after babies and children are making a vital contribution to the economy of the future by preparing a new generation of workers – this vital job is unpaid, of course!

To qualify for the legal right to return in any case, you will remember, a women has to have two years continuous service with her current employer clocked up by the time she gets to eleven weeks before her baby is due and she must have been working sixteen hours a week at least (eight hours a week if she has been in the job five years or more). She also has to tell her employer before she gives up work that she does intend to return to work, and notify the employer three weeks in advance of going back. The Employment Act has added another formality to this whole procedure – the employer can write to the woman at any time later than seven weeks after the expected date of birth and ask if she still intends to return. If she doesn't reply within fourteen days, she loses her rights. Think about this for a moment. The first few weeks after a baby is born are usually pretty chaotic. Lots of women are still recovering from the birth and may have physical or psychological problems apart from being frantically busy trying to organize a new household routine. Would you be at your most efficient, and get your letter back promptly? And how would you get hold of your union representative for advice if the only time you see her or him is at work?

Unions should advise women members that unless they are absolutely positive that they will not in any circumstances want to return they should say that they do want to return whenever the employer asks. Perhaps a couple of examples will illustrate this.

One case involved a woman who was having a child rather late in life. She had been warned of the risks of handicap in babies born to older women and felt she could not promise to return to work. She told her employer she might want to return to work, but could not be sure. The baby was born normal and she herself felt well, so she asked for her job back – the employer refused, saying she had not said she intended to return. She took the employer to an industrial tribunal, which decided she had given away her rights by not saying definitely that she intended to return.

Other examples can be even sadder. Women who miscarry late in pregnancy or have a still birth may well want to return to work even if they would not have returned if things had gone better. A cot death can also result in a woman wanting her job back. And any woman who is intending to return to work keeps her redundancy rights which will at least mean redundancy pay if her job is made redundant.

But the legal right to return is not the same as job security. For a start, not all working women qualify for this right. On top of this many women might not want to return to work with a six-month-old baby, preferring a year or two years leave (a right in many European countries). Women who worked full time before the birth might prefer to return to work part time; there is no right to do this. Most importantly, there is no point at all in the right to return to work if there is no one to look after the child – and this may well be the case.

## Childcare

Throughout the late seventies we have seen cutbacks in public services of all kinds. Let's look at the effects of cuts on care and education for pre-school children. You may know already the answers to these questions for your own area but if not, it's worth finding out.

● Are any new buildings intended for pre-school children standing empty because there is no money to staff them? Or are any buildings of this kind being underused as a result of staffing cuts?
● How many children in your area get the chance to attend nursery school? At what age and for how long?
● How many day nurseries are there in your area? Do you

have to be a single parent or have some other 'problem' before you can get your child into a day nursery? How long are the waiting lists?
- Are there many play-groups? What hours do they run for? Do parents have to take a turn at a rota? Do any of the play groups get grants or other help from public money?
- How many registered childminders are on your local Social Work Department's list? Do you think lots of people in your area use unregistered childminders?
- Do any big factories or offices have childcare facilities for their workers' children?

If nothing else, asking these questions may help to clarify the wide range of different kinds of childcare:-
   nursery schools
   day nurseries
   childminders (registered and unregistered)
   play-groups
   private nurseries
   workplace crèches

The question may also have led you to find out that there are not enough places providing good childcare at the right hours for women who want to go out to work. Day nurseries and childminders, plus workplace crèches if you're lucky, are the only places that look after really young babies and toddlers and usually their hours are long enough to allow parents to go out to work. (Some private nurseries may also care for the youngest children and provide long hours.) Local social work departments keep an eye on all these – they directly control the day nurseries and check up on standards of care at private and workplace nurseries and by child-minders – they also register those they think do provide reasonable childcare.

But one thing you may have found out is that many work-ing parents have to rely on unregistered childminders. Some-times these people may provide a really good service – but there are awful stories of children packed into rooms with no toys, little adult supervision and sometimes real safety hazards like open fires and paraffin heaters. It's an indication of how desperate parents are for childcare that they are prepared to leave their children with – and pay for – a bad childminder. Day nurseries in your area will probably demand that users show they are in real need – whatever that means – and even then waiting lists may be very long.

Play-groups – also watched over by social work departments – and nursery schools and classes, which are under the control of education departments and authorities, generally have as their main priority the needs of the children – who will mostly be aged over two and a half (play-groups) or three (nursery schools and nursery classes attached to primary schools). Play-groups emphasize learning through play, and encourage mothers (not usually fathers) to come to the play-groups and take turns on the rota. They stress the importance of parental involvement, and take pride in educating parents to be 'better' parents. Play-groups don't usually run for longer than three hours a day and this, combined with pressure on parents to take a turn on the rota, tends to make working parents less able to send their children. Nursery schools and nursery classes are also more geared to the needs of the child and although parental involvement isn't required, the hours are pretty short; if parents are expected to collect their children at lunchtime, or only send them for a half-day at a time, going to work is still awkward.

Leaving aside the fact that in the present economic climate we're unlikely to see an expansion of childcare facilities, what sort of childcare would you most like to see provided? Where should childcare be provided – in the community where the children live, or at the workplace? If it's at work, should the employer pay for and control the facilities? Let's have a look at some of the arguments.

● Childcare facilities should be available to everyone and provided out of public funds.
● Childcare should be provided at work so that parents can visit their children at tea-breaks and lunch-breaks, and not have to travel to leave children in care as well as get to work.

- The right to childcare should not depend on whether or not the parent is working.
- Employers get a lot more power over their workers by providing crèches. No one wants to lose their job if that means losing childcare facilities or unsettling a child by moving her or him to a new crèche.
- Childcare should be directly under the control of parents.
- A worker who needs to breastfeed a child can only do so if childcare is provided very near her work.

Which of these arguments do you think are the most important? Which will give the best service to parents and the best care for their children? Your answer will probably depend on your own priorities. The TUC's answer, in their booklet the 'TUC Charter on Facilities for the Under Five's', comes out in favour of a national system of childcare based on local nursery centres providing for the educational, welfare and health needs of pre-school children and linked to local play-groups and childminders. The booklet stresses the importance of choice for parents about whether to go out to work or stay at home and care for children – and points out that this choice cannot be a real choice until parents can be provided with either financial security to stay at home, or with free, good quality childcare, operating during flexible hours and available on demand to anyone who wishes for it.

The TUC also stresses the importance of the terms and conditions on which a parent is employed. Maternity leave we have already looked at, and there is plenty of scope for improvement in the law there. Paternity leave would be of great help to families around the time of birth of a child. An entitlement to take time off to care for sick children is as important to a working parent as the right to take sick leave her or himself.

Parents with school-age children still face problems in combining childcare with work. Sickness, school holidays, and the fact that most people's working days are longer than the hours their children are at school all present problems. Children are not supervised at lunchtimes in Scottish schools and school meals are rising in cost and declining in quality. In a few areas, some steps have been taken to improve after-school care, and play-schemes during at least part of the school holidays can help parents over that particular problem. Cutbacks in public spending make it less and less likely that lunchtime, after-school and school holiday childcare will be provided. Will this mean more and more parents (mothers) being forced to give up paid work? Or losing their jobs for absenteeism?

## The right to choose

Our lives at home do affect our lives at work. We have seen already how housework and responsibility for childcare affect us. Perhaps it's worth having a look at the choice of whether or not to have children before we try to sum up the effects of domestic responsibilities on our working lives. Once again, we have to look at whether this is a real choice, or whether there are strings attached. The most obvious constraint is probably money. Children have to be kept and apart from that childcare, or the lack of it, will affect every parents chance of finding work or getting good wages. Lots of families feel they can't afford to have children. Should this be an issue for trade unions?

For those who don't want to have children there isn't a free choice either. Unless you decide to give up your sex life, you are a lesbian or infertile, you take the risk of getting pregnant if you are a woman. Contraception may have improved a lot this century, but it's still a bit primitive.

- You can take the Pill, run very little risk of pregnancy, but take a chance on whether you feel fine or rotten, and also take a small chance with your life.
- You can use an IUD (intra uterine device, coil, loop, copper 7) run a slightly greater risk of pregnancy, risk infection and heavy periods – and once again take a very small chance with your life.
- You can use the good old-fashioned barrier methods – the sheath, the cap or diaphragm – and take no risk with your life, but a greater risk of pregnancy.

60

● Or you can say you can't be bothered with all this equipment and just take the risk you'll get pregnant.

Whichever way you play it, you may end up pregnant when you didn't plan to be. Is this a trade union issue? Is it anything to do with us as trade unionists that the inadequacy of contraception leads to trade union members getting pregnant when they didn't want to be – and may eventually affect members working lives?

The whole issue of the availability of abortion comes in here as well. As trade unionists, should we have a point of view on the issue of a woman's right to choose whether she does or does not want an abortion and on the availability of NHS abortions to those women who want them? It is an issue which affects trade union members' lives, and which, in a society which does not provide enough childcare, is bound to affect members' chances at work. Does that make it something on which unions should have policies?

## The women worker – paid and unpaid

In this chapter we have looked at the way things are, rather than the way to change them. Let's try to sum up what we have said about women's two jobs, paid or unpaid. Perhaps you would like to look back at the questions outlined at the beginning of the chapter, to see if we have thrown any light on the issues involved.

We have already looked at:

● The way the family and government policies both affect women's lives at work – and the working lives of men who are responsible for housework and childcare.
● Whether women can ever be treated the same as men at work while the family and goverment attitudes to the family remain unchanged.
● What trade unions have to think about if the interests of members who are also parents and houseworkers are to be genuinely taken into account.

The thing we will need to do next is to try to work out what all this has to do with womens rights at work and tackle the way trade unions might be able to make changes for the better. We will tackle these problems again later, but we are already in a position to start thinking about these questions:

● Does the family get in the way of women getting their rights at work? If so, is the solution to get rid of the family, to change who does what in the family, or to change the way the state treats the family? Or is the family not the problem at all, and is the answer changes at work – everything from equal pay to more flexible working hours for both men and women?
● What are the problems for trade unions if many workers are parents too? How can the unions best organize working parents? Should the trade unions have a point of view on domestic responsibilities or are they poking their noses into people's private affairs?

## Further reading

'The Hidden Army' Simon Crine (Low Pay Unit, 1979). This pamphlet describes the predicament of homeworkers, and makes suggestions about what could be done to help improve their conditions.

*Woman at Work* Jenny Glew (Pitman, 1979). A handbook for women either starting work or going back to work. It discusses the difficulties of combining domestic responsibilities with a job, as well as outlining the kinds of jobs women do, and women's rights at work. It's very straightforward, and gives a lot of practical information.

*The Gender Trap Book 2: Sex and marriage* Carol Adams and Rae Laurikietus, (Virago, 1980.) From the same series as the book *Education and Work* mentioned at the end of Chapter one, this book deals with some of the basic arguments about woman's role in the home.

The National Council for Civil Liberties have a Rights for Women Unit who put out a fair number of pamphlets and books on the areas we have looked at in this chapter. 'The Unequal Breadwinner, a new perspective on women and Social Security' by Ruth Lister and Leo Wilson (NCCL, 1976), 'Income Tax and Sex Discrimination' by Patricia Hewitt (NCCL, 1979), and 'Maternity Rights for Working Women' by Jean Coussins, 2nd edition (NCCL, 1980), are all full of useful and well-presented information – and don't take long to read.

*Equality for some*, the tape-study pack mentioned in the further reading for Chapter one, is relevant here as well.

'Women under attack' (Counter Information Services Report No. 15), was produced when the Labour Government introduced the first round of cuts in the public services in the mid seventies. It describes how cutbacks affect women both as workers in the public services, and as users of childcare, schools, old people's homes, and hospitals. A new CIS report, 'Women in the 80s', updates this information.

*Women and the Welfare State* Elizabeth Wilson (Tavistock, 1977) gives a lot more detail on how women fit into the Welfare State.

'TUC Charter on the under-fives' (TUC, 1978) summarizes the findings of a TUC working party, and outlines a policy for a long-term national policy on childcare and some suggestions for stopgap measures. It covers a lot of ground in just a few pages.

'Workplace Nurseries – a negotiating kit' (NALGO, 1979/80), is much more than just a leaflet about workplace nurseries. It isn't long, but it does go into practical details and looks at the broader policy issues for trade unions. It describes what has already been done, and how well various attempts are working – both in the area of setting up crèches, and in parents' rights at work.

The Equal Opportunities Commission regularly produces reports on childcare, income tax, public services, low pay, the pension age, and so on. Write for a list of their publications, which are usually free. Their address: EOC, Overseas House, Quay Street, Manchester M3 3HN.

*Health and Safety at Work* by Dave Eva and Ron Oswald (Pan, 1981) looks at workers' health. It's worth reading, keeping in mind that women also do another unpaid job at home.

# Chapter **Three**

# 'Now that you've got equality ...'

In the last two chapters we have looked at the work women do, at the difficulties girls and women face in education and training, and at what it's like trying to combine going out to work with domestic responsibilities. Can the problems we have talked about be solved by changes in the law? In fact, are they already on the way to being solved by the Equal Pay Act, the Sex Discrimination Act, and the law on maternity rights? What do the laws we have actually say? Do they work? Do we need more laws? Do we need to see some other kind of action?

In this chapter we will be talking about:

- protective legislation;
- the Equal Pay Act;
- the Sex Discrimination Act;
- part-time workers rights.

## Equality and the law

When the first women won the vote, lots of suffragettes must have got very fed up with people saying to them 'Well, you'll be happy now you've got the vote. Women are equal now.' Fifty years later women activists were bristling at the same words, only this time 'equal pay' was substituted for 'the vote'. Five years later the same old comment was still being trotted out – this time 'this Sex Discrimination Act' was going to give women equality.

The women who've muttered crossly back, 'we've always *been* equal' at different times this century have always had a bit of trouble getting their point across. No piece of law can ever make people equal – what it can give is equal rights. And no law this century has yet given women equal rights even though there have been a growing number of people prepared to say we were born equal.

Trade unions have been mouthing demands for equal pay for more than a century and struggles around specific women's rights issues have been a feature of the labour movement throughout its history. Yet women's rights have always been regarded as something of a side issue within trade unions – surprising as men's political rights have always been hotly debated throughout trade union history. We'll return to this later, but let's look first at how any legal change actually comes to have an effect on us in our daily lives.

### What does having a law mean?

Have you ever heard anyone say 'You can't do that – it's illegal!' or 'I'm sure he doesn't have the right to do that'? Both of these comments show that we all know that people do things which are against the law – and sometimes get away with it. Just because we have a particular law doesn't mean nobody breaks it. (None of us are allowed by law to park on double yellow lines – but you can often see cars, vans and lorries parked there all the same.) Laws are no good unless they are enforced, and unless the courts interpret the laws as the law-makers intended.

We are all familiar with the idea that the police are responsible for catching people who break the *criminal* law. But the police are not going to come to your workplace to see if your employer is paying you the right wages under the Equal Pay Act or treating you fairly under the Sex Discrimination Act. Why not? Because both these Acts are part of the *civil* law – the kind of law any of us can use to get compensation for losses we suffer as a result of someone else's actions. For example, if the people who live upstairs leave on their bath taps and water comes through your ceiling and damages your property you could take them to court. If the only damage is to the paintwork on your ceiling you almost certainly won't bother – although *in law* you could go to court to try and reclaim the cost of a pot of paint from your upstairs neighbours. But the fact that you have a legal right to claim from your upstairs neighbour doesn't mean that someone stops your neighbour leaving the taps on – just that there is a legal way you can get the cost of your losses back.

It's the same with, for example, the Equal Pay Act. You can go to an industrial tribunal to claim your legal rights – and even go on to the Employment Appeal Tribunal and the House of Lords if you think the industrial tribunal hasn't made the correct decision. The fact that you *could* do this will encourage your employer to abide by the law – but so would a collective agreement between the employer and the trade unions at the workplace.

The *criminal* law does have something to do with women's rights at work too. The Health and Safety at Work Act, and various other laws on safety at work are criminal laws – though here it's the factory inspector or one of the other inspectors employed by the Health and Safety Executive rather than the police who are responsible for catching lawbreakers. Minimum wages are enforced by wages inspectors

– again breaking the law is a criminal offence, and can lead to a fine. Even though these are criminal laws, employers still break them.

The point here is that laws don't *stop* anyone doing anything – they just introduce penalties for those who are caught, or who have a claim made against them. While you are reading about women's legal rights at work, keep in mind that the law will only work if employers are not prepared to risk the consequences of breaking the law. Collective agreements between employers and trade unions work when the employer – or the union – is not prepared to risk the consequences of breaking the agreement. Which do you think would work best – the law or agreements? While you are reading about women's legal rights at work, keep this question in mind and think too about whether an industrial tribunal or your trade union would be more likely to help you get equal pay or fair treatment.

## The protective laws

These laws, some of which date back to the middle of the last century, take a totally different approach to the problems of women at work from the more recent laws on equality. Let's look at them first and see the approach taken to women workers in the past.

The protective laws are the ones that give women special protection from certain hazardous processes at work, for example working with lead, and make night work illegal in factories unless various conditions are met. Most of these laws were the result of campaigns by trade unionists and reformers to improve the dreadful conditions in which many women worked last century. Are they out of date today, now women are pressing for equal treatment at work? Did these laws ever really help women? Do they help women now?

Let's look at why these laws were passed in the first place. Public opinion had been outraged by the results of government inquiries into the working conditions of women and young people in factories and in the mining industry. Some

67

of the reports showed more concern for morality than for the workers' health. This comes out in two ways – a concern that women working long hours would cause a deterioration in family life, and the worry that morals would be undermined by the sexes working 'half-naked' in close proximity under ground. You will notice that the woman's role in the home is one of the reasons for banning long hours of work for her, but not for her husband – wasn't he expected to take part in family life? Is the underlying assumption once again that women should really be at home doing the housework? No one looked very hard at *why* women worked long hours in the first place. Did women have so much time on their hands after caring for their homes and children that they wanted to work long hours? What do you think made them do it? What about low pay as an answer? The women certainly were low paid. But why didn't the reformers see the solution in raising wages? And why didn't the trade unions think in these terms, rather than throwing their weight behind demands for legislation to limit hours?

Women workers themselves protested at the time. To them, all the laws meant was that they could no longer earn enough for their families to live on. Many felt male trade unionists had supported the laws limiting hours of work just to get women out of the labour market – which would of course increase men's bargaining power with employers by creating a labour shortage. They felt the same applied to getting women out of the pits. Do you think they were right?

Let's get back to the present day. The laws are a bit of a mess at the moment, and the Equal Opportunities Commission has produced a report on them, recommending that they are repealed. Do you think this is the right answer? There are two opposing arguments being put forward in the trade unions at the moment. Let's summarize them.

The first argument goes like this. Trade unions have won an important right for some women workers not to do night work; why should we give up this right without a struggle, and just throw a hard-won concession away? We should fight for the extension of these laws to men too, so that no one has to do night work.

The second argument goes this way. Employers use the fact that women can't do night work to keep women's pay down and restrict the choice of jobs open to them, and unions go along with this when it helps to keep men's rates high or keep women out of 'men's' jobs. So in a factory where men and women do the same jobs at different times of day, the union can keep the men happy by negotiating high premiums for night shift, and the women on the basic rate stay low paid. If the women complain, they are told its the fault of the law. So the employer keeps his cheap labour, the men get reasonable pay, and the women suffer because their trade union organization is weak.

Which argument convinces you? Or can you see some truth in both? There is one more problem. Lots of women who do night work in hospitals, or cleaning offices are not covered by law. More and more factories too are being given permission to employ women on the night shift. Should the laws on night work be extended to cover all women, and perhaps all men (as they do in Scandinavia except for a few specified jobs), or should we get rid of them? Women workers in practice often have to do a second job as a housewife and mother, like Rita, who operates a machine which prepares the fish you buy in cans at your local supermarket. Fish canneries are allowed to employ women at night because fish are perishable.

'I had to go back to work six weeks after my first baby was born. We couldn't have managed otherwise. I did nights at the fish factory while my man watched the baby. I got home just before he left for work at the engineering factory. He had to do overtime too, so we didn't see much of each other.'

What would have been the most help to Rita and her family? Laws that meant she couldn't work all night and then spend the day doing housework and looking after a child as well as trying to get some sleep, or better wages for the hours she did at work, or better wages for her husband? What should we as trade unionists do to improve the situation of workers like Rita?

The other aspect of protective legislation applies to hazards at work, and perhaps it's not so different to see an easy answer here. In the area of health hazards women do face special problems.

As we have already seen, expectant mothers may be at extra risk themselves, as well as the extra risk to an unborn child; and a woman may not realize she is pregnant for a few weeks. Apart from this, some hazards, for example vibration, are known to affect women much worse than men. Threshold limit values – official figures which recommend maximum exposures to chemicals – are worked out on the basis of men's body weight. The same amount of poison has a very much greater effect in the body of a small person than in a large person – and women's average weight is much less than men's. Of course, here, smaller than average men and boys are at extra risk too, and safety representatives should always keep this in mind. Special legislation which takes account of the particular problems of one sex can be a good thing – for men too, of course, if men are found to be more sensitive to particular substances than women. Our objective as trade unionists should always be to improve conditions – we must look at each situation to see how best to do this. The Health and Safety at Work Act gives a base from which we can work to improve all workers' safety and health – we should use it effectively. You can read more about this in *Health and Safety at Work*, another book in this series.

Now let's go on to some more recent laws, and see if they do any better at helping women workers.

## The Equal Pay Act

What does the Equal Pay Act say? Will it solve the problem of low pay? The Equal Pay Act says that men and women should be treated the same for doing the same job, providing there is not some other reason – nothing to do with their sex – why they should be treated differently.

The Equal Pay Act doesn't just refer to pay – it gives the right to be treated the same as someone of the opposite sex in relation to all sorts of other terms and conditions of employment too. To take some practical examples, the number of days holiday allowed, the right to luncheon vouchers or use of a subsidized canteen, access to pension schemes, and all sorts of perks are covered by the Act. In legal terms everything covered by the Contract of Employment between the employer and the employee is covered by the Equal Pay Act, and neither a man nor a woman can be treated less favourably than another employee of the opposite sex under the Act. (It's important to remember, though, that it's not just things which are written down which form the Contract of Employment in law – all sorts of agreed and accepted practices also become part of what a lawyer would describe as the contract.)

But you will remember that in 1980 women were still not earning the same as men. Women's hourly rates had managed to reach an all-time high of around two-thirds of men's hourly rates in 1977–8, and had then started to fall behind again. The Equal Pay Act was passed in 1970, came into full operation in 1975, and hadn't changed anything very much by 1980. What had happened? Let's look at some of the words we used to describe the Act a bit more carefully. Men and women should be treated *the same* for doing *the same job*, providing there is not *some other reason* for the difference in pay.

This means you must find another employee of the opposite sex to compare yourself with before you can claim equal treatment – quite a problem sometimes. Two people's idea of what constitutes the same job can vary a lot. A woman or man can only claim equal treatment with someone of the opposite sex under the Act if she or he can show, in the words of the Act, that she or he is doing 'like work' or that the work has been given the same value under a job evaluation scheme.

'Like work' is defined by the Act to mean either the same job, or a job which is 'broadly similar' to the job which has been chosen for comparison, and which is not different in ways which are of 'practical importance'. It's easier to understand what this means if we take an example. A woman and a man work in a warehouse, doing much the same things

– taking things to and from the shelves, keeping track of what is in stock, and dealing with enquiries. Most Monday mornings a few things have accumulated for deliveries and a few general errands have to be run. The man usually gets these out of the road then, as there is often a spare van around on Monday mornings. The woman, on the other hand, although she can drive, doesn't do deliveries – she has another special job, typing up the warehouse records, which takes her part of most Friday afternoons.

Looking at this example, are the jobs 'like work'? Only if we decide that the jobs are the same or broadly similar to each other, and if the jobs are not the same, then any differences between the jobs must not be of 'practical importance'. In our example the jobs are not the same, so we can't show 'like work' this way. But the two jobs do seem quite similar – both people spend most of their time doing the same kind of work, so perhaps there is a chance to establish 'like work' by showing that the jobs are 'broadly similar' and that differences between the jobs are not of 'practical importance'. If they are not, then the two jobs have been shown to be 'like work', and a claim for equal treatment would get through this first stage.

The other way to get through the first stage is to show that the two jobs have equal value. 'Great,' you may be saying, 'I'm sure my job is as valuable as lots of the men's jobs around here.' Unfortunately, the Act goes on to define 'equal value' as 'having been given the same grade on a job evaluation scheme' – which is not quite the same thing. Job evaluation is said to be a scientific way of deciding who should be paid the most. How much faith do you have in job evaluation? Let's look at what it is and why it's used.

The most common kind of job evaluation scheme awards every job a certain number of points for, say, the length of training needed or the amount of physical strength required, or the level of responsibility involved. All the points awarded to each job are added up, and people with around the same number of points are put on the same grade, which then sets their rate of pay. A practical – though very oversimplified – example of this might be a woman weaver and a male labourer in a textile factory. The woman's job might get five points for the training she has done, and two points for responsibility, and no points for physical strength. The man's job might get six points for physical strength, no points for training and one point for responsibility. Both jobs – if these were the only things taken into account – would end up with seven points, and so fall into the same grade. So in this case, a comparison for equal treatment can be made between jobs which are quite different – weaving and labouring – because they have been given the same grade under a job evaluation scheme.

But a claim for equal treatment doesn't end there. Once you have proved 'like work' you still have to get through another stage – showing that there isn't some reason – other than sex – why a particular man and woman should be treated differently. This kind of other reason is known in the Act as a 'material difference', and once again, an example will probably make it easier for you to see what this means in practice. A man and a woman work in a local government office dealing with the public and answering telephone enquiries. He gets paid nearly half as much again as she does, but he is in his forties, and has been with the council twenty years, and she is in her twenties and has been with the council four years.

Here there is probably no question that they are both doing the same job, and 'like work' is easy to establish. But there are two other big differences between them – their ages and their length of service. Both age and length of service usually count towards better pay in this type of work, and both are the sort of thing the Act is referring to in the words 'material difference'.

So just to go back once more, the Equal Pay Act says if you do the 'like work' you are entitled to the same pay and conditions unless there is a relevant 'material difference'.

What an Act says is not enough on its own. We have to know whether employers are abiding by the Act, and what the legal system says before we really get a clear idea of its impact.

**The employers respond – trade unions outmanoeuvred** The Equal Pay Act 1970 did not come into force until December 1975. These five years were supposed to ensure that Equal Pay got off to a flying start, with all employers abiding by the law as soon as it came in, and plenty of time to work out well in advance any problems caused by the advent of Equal Pay.

Certainly employers did put their minds to the Equal Pay Act well in advance – but to a rather different purpose. Equal pay was going to cost a lot of money. Special 'men's rates' and 'women's rates' were common, and it was quite obvious that no man was going to take a cut in wages to the women's rate.

Did employers spend those five years working out ways to avoid the impact of equal pay – and swindle women workers out of their legal entitlements? The employers who thought hardest were those in industries which employed a lot of women. Here is an example of their lines of thought from *Catering and Hotel Management*, a magazine read by many managers in catering.

The solution to the new legislation is not simply raising women's wages to those of men employees. In one instance in a similarly female labour-intensive industry, rapid calculation suggested that this approach would cost an additional £100,000 . . . However, guidance can often be found in job evaluation and when this was applied in this instance the cost was reduced to around £10,000.

How can this be done? Job evaluation is supposed to be a *fairer* way of paying wages, based on looking at what each job requires of each employee. You will remember the way job evaluation gives points for various aspects of a job. Now think about what would happen in practice – remembering the differences between 'men's work' and 'women's work' – if we used this system.

|  | *maximum score* |
|---|---|
| physical strength | 10 |
| allowance for dirty work | 10 |
| length of training | 10 |
| manual dexterity | 3 |
| monotonous work | 3 |

Men's work would, of course, get more points on average than women's work. Even if you get the full points allowance for dexterity, you are only doing as well as someone who gets three out of ten for physical strength required to do the job.

People who work out job evaluation schemes live in the same world as the rest of us. They know they would never get any men to apply for a labourer's job if they only offered the same grade – and therefore rate of pay – as women would be prepared to take, often for quite a skilled job. So if the job evaluation scheme ends up recommending that the women get paid more than the men, it's pretty likely to get thrown back to the person who drew it up, with instructions to come up with a new scheme that will actually work. The easiest way to change things around is to look at the skills the women have, and give them a low maximum score (e.g. three for dexterity) and to look at the skills men have and given them a high score (e.g. ten for physical strength). Of course, you could do exactly the same in reverse to end up with good wages for women's work and bad wages for men's work – but there don't seem to be many examples!

Job evaluation isn't the only thing employers did to get ready for December 1975 and the Act coming in. A study done for the Department of Employment on the way twenty-five employers responded to the Equal Pay Act showed that eleven of the twenty-five were guilty of working out ways to avoid the full cost of equal pay. Three main ideas were used – job evaluation, which we have already looked at; job segregation; and unisex pay scales.

Job segregation was simply a matter of making sure men and women didn't do the same jobs – you will remember you have to find another employee of your firm doing the same job before you can claim equal treatment. If all the women just happen to work on the production line, and all the men just happen to be labourers, or all the women work in the office and all the men on the shop-floor, there can be no claims under the law for equal pay. (But there might be under the Sex Discrimination Act, which we'll be coming to later.) So rather than pay a man's rate and a woman's rate, you have jobs which men do and jobs which women do, and you pay different rates for the different jobs.

Unisex pay scales look terrific. Several grades may be listed, there is a rate for each grade, or sometimes a scale for each grade. But if you see a unisex pay system, ask how many men and how many women get paid what. Two things may happen. You may find all the women in the lower grades and all the men in the top ones, or you may find that within each grade, women are on the lower points of the wage scales, and men at the top. Either way, equal pay may have been very neatly sidestepped. You need quite detailed information on pay to show that the women *are* ending up worse off than the men, so it can be quite difficult to challenge the way men and women are paid differently.

Employers, then, used their time wisely to avoid a good deal of the cost of complying with the Equal Pay Act. Unfortunately trade unions were not quick enough to respond to the employers' tricks; unions had not worked out tactics to deal with job evaluation schemes being used to keep down women's pay. It is a lesson to us to realize the same Department of Employment study found unions had collaborated with management in drawing up discriminatory job evaluation schemes in 60 per cent of cases where job evaluation was used. This is perhaps understandable when you think of the pressures negotiators are under from their members. Male workers would have kicked up a hell of a fuss if women had been given big increases while the men got nothing – even if it was all in the name of equal pay. What do you think of the unions' behaviour?

## The Equal Pay Act in practice

Once the Equal Pay Act was tested out in the industrial tribunals and the Employment Appeal Tribunal it became even clearer that this might not turn out to be women's dream come true. Briefly, 'broadly similar' was interpreted as 'almost exactly the same', the most trivial differences between jobs turned out to be 'differences of practical importance', job evaluation schemes had been worked out in a way that appeared fair – though coincidentally women seemed to end up at the bottom rather a lot, and 'material differences' of all kinds were accepted as reasons for different treatment of men and women. You can read up on the details of this in 'The Equality Report' produced by the National Council for Civil Liberties and 'The Equal Pay and Sex Discrimination Acts – Report from Scotland' published by Aberdeen People's Press.

## The Central Arbitration Committee

The Central Arbitration Committee, who enforce the Equal Pay Act where groups of workers are affected by employers' pay schemes, or by collectively agreed rates of pay, provided one bright spot. They made a brave decision to compare 'women's work' with 'men's work' in one pay award. Foremen and storekeepers were both paid more than any of the office staff in one firm, although one of the office staff had responsibility for supervising the other workers and another member of office staff had considerable responsibility as an assistant to a manager. The CAC awarded these two senior office workers equal pay with the foremen, on the grounds that they had equivalent levels of responsibility – and experienced adult office staff were awarded equal pay with the storemen. This is a significant step towards regarding 'equal pay for work of equal value' as a guiding principle, rather than 'equal pay for the same work'. But a Court of Appeal decision has now prevented this kind of decision being taken again.

## When should Equal Pay be awarded?

The problem of what equal pay should be awarded for has been a major stumbling block. Whilst women do different kinds of work from men – as we saw in the first chapter – equal pay for the same work is not going to get women very far – most women would have problems finding a man doing the same job. The use of job evaluation in the Equal Pay Act to provide a comparison of 'work of equal value' will continue to be a pretty hollow comparison as long as women's skills are less highly valued than men's – and this will be the case until women cease to be willing to work for less than men. Until this time too, trade union response may be a bit half-hearted – for reasons we will be discussing in the next chapter.

## The Sex Discrimination Act

In the five years between the Equal Pay Act getting through Parliament and coming into force, pressure grew for a Sex Discrimination Act, as workers became more aware that the Equal Pay Act would merely shunt women off into different jobs from men – and discrimination would keep certain jobs as 'men's' and others as 'women's' so that there would never be a basis for an equal pay comparison. The Sex Discrimination Act came into force in late December 1975.

Various forms of legislation had been discussed in the early seventies and the Sex Discrimination Act in its final form was quite an improvement on some of the earlier versions. One of the most important improvements was to introduce the idea of 'indirect discrimination'; another was to make it possible to take 'positive action'. But the Act is still far from perfect, as we will see.

First of all, the Act makes it illegal to discriminate between people at work and treat some worse than others because of their sex. This discrimination is not lawful whether it is *direct* or *indirect*.

*Direct* discrimination happens when a woman is treated worse than a man on the grounds that she is a woman (or vice versa).

*Indirect* discrimination happens when, for example, an employer's training scheme only offers places to people who are under twenty-six. On the face of it, this is nothing to do with sex. But if you look at the typical working life of women, you will find that many women take a break from paid work during their twenties to bring up children. This will make it considerably more difficult in general for women to apply for the training scheme, and unless the employer can show that being less than twenty-six really is crucial to the job, women denied access to the scheme will be able to complain of indirect discrimination.

Another example would be if a posh restaurant advertised for waiters/waitresses over six feet tall. As height has nothing to do with the ability to do this job, and as this rule will make it considerably more difficult for women than men to get the job, this too would be indirect discrimination.

## Marriage Discrimination

The Sex Discrimination Act also makes it illegal to treat some-one who is married worse than someone who is single in matters to do with employment. (But notice that sex discrimi-nation applies to education, provision of goods and services and housing as well as to work.) This time there isn't a clause the other way round – it *is* legal to treat someone worse because they are single, but the same ideas about direct and indirect discrimination apply.

This time *direct* discrimination refers to treating someone worse simply because she or he is married. *Indirect* marriage discrimination would occur if an employer refused to employ anyone who had children. This would make it considerably more difficult for married people than for single people to get a job, and married people who didn't get a job as a result of this employer's policy would be able to complain. Matters to do with employment are covered right from the time you apply for a job. Employers complained that the Sex Discrimi-nation Act had interfered with one of their most important freedoms – to be able to hire whoever they liked. Employers had always been able to refuse to take on a perfectly well-qualified applicant for a job – simply because they didn't like that person, because they had always refused to take on people with red hair, or because someone had been black-listed. With the Sex Discrimination Act, and later the Race Discrimination Act, this freedom was limited – applicants for jobs had to be treated fairly, at least in terms of sex and race. If an employer wouldn't take on women, or wouldn't take on Asians, the company could be forced to pay some compensation to the people who had been denied jobs. Do you think this is an interference with employers' freedom? If so is it justified? Or would you go further and demand that employers should be forced not to operate blacklists, or let their prejudices interfere in any way with who gets jobs? (Some unions, for example printers in London, have managed to achieve this by agreement – any vacant job must be given to the first union member who applies.)

Lots of people and organizations wrote to their MPs in 1974 to say the Act would not work if women were frightened to use it, and they suggested that there should be protection from victimization in the Act. This was eventually included, so that women who took action under the Act would have legal protection from losing their jobs or being treated badly at work.

That gives you an outline of the main principles of the Act. You can get more detail from a free booklet published by the Equal Opportunities Commission called 'Sex Discrimination – A guide to the Sex Discrimination Act 1975'. Make sure you get the full guide, not one of the short three or four page versions. From the outline we have looked at so far, do you think the Act will have contributed much towards solving the problems we talked about in the first two chapters? What do you think might be wrong with the Act? Take a while to think about it.

Now think back to what we have said before about the work that women do and how different it is from 'men's work'. Remember also that there has been no dramatic change in the kinds of work that women do since 1975. Would you have expected a change? Why do you think nothing very noticeable has happened? Let's list some of the possible reasons and then look at each one and see if it seems likely. (Add your own ideas to the list too.)

● The Sex Discrimination Act is badly worded.
● The tribunals are interpreting the Act in such a way that there is very little need for changes in the way employers treat women.

- Few people are prepared to take cases to tribunals, or demand that the law is enforced in their own workplace.
- Only a few people know about the law.
- People have no faith in the Act and choose to ignore it.
- The fact that there haven't been major changes shows that the Act wasn't ever necessary – employers have always chosen the best person for the job, and it just shows men really are better at some kinds of work and women at others – and that men's work is more valuable and therefore better paid.
- The Sex Discrimination Act was all very fine in its own way, but didn't really get at the main problems facing women at work.
- You just can't change some things, like the way women are treated at work, by passing laws.

Let's look at these arguments.

## Is the Act badly worded?

The wording of the Act doesn't seem too bad on the face of it, and it includes the idea of 'indirect discrimination' – which would otherwise have been a massive loophole for employers. But notice it gives no protection to single people – who can, quite legally, be refused a job or promotion simply because they are single. Also, although the Act provides some protection from prejudice against women or against men, it provides no protection from prejudice against lesbians or homosexuals. As the recent case of John Saunders in Scotland shows, employers can sack a worker quite legally if they think other people might be prejudiced against the worker – and it doesn't matter whether or not that worker does his or her job well, or whether the prejudice is justified in any way.

John Saunders worked as a caretaker/handyman in a summer camp for children. He was sacked after an anonymous phone call to his employers tipped them off to the fact that he was gay. Experts were called who said that he was no more likely to interfere with children than a heterosexual person, and the tribunal accepted this evidence.

But they still said that the employers' case that parents would be alarmed – even though their alarm was not well-founded – was enough to justify dismissal.

What do you think of this case? In the Conservative proposals for sex discrimination legislation put out for comment in the early 1970s, the same argument could have been used against women. They suggested that where customers' preferences made it necessary, employers should be allowed to discriminate. This would have meant, for example, that a man could have been refused a job selling cosmetics on the grounds that customers would prefer to buy from a woman. Do you think this would be justified? And do you think the Sex Discrimination Act now covers this area adequately?

The Sex Discrimination Act still allows exceptions – firstly, where there is a *genuine occupational qualification* (GOQ). These GOQs are pretty carefully defined – but allow models and actors to be chosen by sex; along with people whose job requires safeguards for privacy and decency (either because of physical contact or because people are likely to be undressed or using sanitary facilities); people who have to live in remote single-sex accommodation; some people working in certain kinds of schools, hospitals or prisons, or in certain other occupations where personal services are provided to individuals; and people working in jobs where the law restricts what women can do. Work outside the UK in countries which do not like women to do particular jobs is also a special case – and so are jobs where a married couple are required to do two jobs between them.

Are these exceptions too wide or too narrow? Think of an example of discrimination you know about – even if it's just that women somehow seem to end up in the worst paid or lowest grade jobs at some workplace you know of. Would the Sex Discrimination Act be any use to you to get a better deal for women? Keep in mind direct and indirect discrimination (by sex and marriage) and GOQs. Would you say the Act is worded well or badly? What would you change if you wrote the law?

## How have the Tribunals been interpreting the Act?

If you are going to claim your legal rights, you will have to be prepared to go to an industrial tribunal. The tribunals are less formal than a court and instead of a judge and jury, your case will be decided by a chairperson with legal qualifications and two tribunal members – usually one nominated by the CBI (the employers' organization) and one nominated by the TUC (England and Wales) or STUC (Scotland).

The main trouble arises because its up to you to prove your employer – or an employer you wanted a job with – has discriminated against you. How do you get the necessary evidence? For example, if you are a woman and have applied for a job and not got an interview, and you know men you think are no more skilled or better qualified than you who *have* been interviewed, what could you do? You would have to find out who else applied, and what their skills were – this could be tricky enough, even though under section 74 of the Act – the questions procedure – you can write and ask for this kind of information from a company. It's bad enough trying to get this kind of information in the first place, but it's worse when you get to the tribunal. It's usually possible for an employer to find some other reason – apart from being a woman – why you haven't been interviewed, or gained access to a training scheme or a better paid job, or whatever your complaint is.

Tribunals have tended to take the employer's word for it, that there is some other reason rather than assuming sex discrimination – and in terms of the law they are quite correct – it's up to you to prove you have been discriminated against. So lots of people have lost cases because employers said they had inadequate experience, poor educational qualifications in certain subjects, lack of supervisory potential, 'the wrong type of personality for the organization' and so on.

## Do people lack faith in the law or fear to use it?

Most people find it hard to see how the Sex Discrimination Act applies to them and to their own job. Yet many people are in jobs where everyone knows that either women or men stand a better chance of getting any vacancy that comes up and where, in theory, people might be able to use the Act. But it's hard to prove discrimination without facts – sometimes you might even need quite detailed statistics. This is a discouragement in itself.

Quite apart from the difficulty of getting a case together, something else must be stopping people from flooding to the tribunal. Only seven sex discrimination cases were heard in Scotland in the first year of the Act – one was successful. The situation in England and Wales was very similar and all over Britain the number of cases being brought each year is now (1980) going down. (The same thing is true for the Equal Pay Act, too, by the way.)

Why don't many people take cases? Some have heard about the kinds of decisions tribunals have made, and about the ease with which employers can get off the hook by producing other reasons for the way they have behaved. More important, perhaps, is a fear of rocking the boat. The Act may provide protection against victimization, but it's even more difficult to prove than discrimination. It could just be your turn for the worst jobs, or to get away late, or there could be a reason for changing your hours slightly so that picking up your children becomes just that little bit more difficult. And with unemployment rising, whose job is going to go, whose hours are to be cut?

Apart from the kind of tricks your employer can play, your workmates may well think you're off your head to complain about some practice or other that's been going on for years. Would you be keen to try to claim your rights through legal channels? What sort of reaction would you get from your workmates?

Trade unions have been able to get Equal Opportunities agreements with some employers as a guarantee of fair treatment for men and women. Once again this needs to be closely monitored by the unions involved, or else traditions and established practices may reappear, leaving women at the bottom of the heap once again.

*Could any Act solve the main problems facing women at work?*

We have already seen that men and women do different jobs, and that women tend to earn less than men. This hasn't changed since the Sex Discrimination Act became law. Is this, as some people say, because women really have different skills – and less valuable skills at that? If that were true, it would explain the present situation quite well – it would only be logical that men still earn more. But we looked in Chapter two at how certain jobs get the label of skilled and found out this didn't just depend on the real level of skill involved, but also on demand for workers, trade union organization and so on.

The question really is, can the Sex Discrimination Act challenge the structure of wages? In other words, can our notions of the skill involved in certain kinds of work, or the value of some jobs be looked at differently with the aid of the Act? Or are the ideas of skill and value that we have learnt during our past working lives so strong that no Act can change the way we think? We come back to two ideas we have looked at already:

● the way we are educated and trained and the things we expect for women and men.

*and*

● one of the questions we left hanging at the end of Chapter two – family responsibilities and changes at work.

The first idea is possibly one explanation of why we often don't see as problems things which would be covered by the Sex Discrimination Act if it was working properly – girls just don't come foward in large numbers for jobs in engineering and construction and most boys don't want to be typists or cleaners. Neither sex is fighting for the recognition of typing or cleaning as a skill, though typing has become an essential part of the new phototypesetting work now being used on local and national newspapers from *The Times* to the Aberdeen *Press and Journal*. There is more to typesetting than just typing, but will the fact that the mostly male, one-time hot

85

metal typesetters now sit at a keyboard make *their* jobs easier to define as 'women's work', and therefore less skilled and lower paid in the future? Some of them must be worried that the employers will begin to think this way.

The second idea – family responsibilities – is another crucial factor. Part-time work is only available in certain kinds of jobs and, whilst many women responsible for running a family opt for part-time paid work, women will stay in traditional jobs, however much opportunity to take up other *full-time* work is offered – unless employers actually try to get women into traditional male jobs and provide part-time opportunities. This may actually be in the employer's interests in some cases – particularly if labour costs can be reduced this way.

The Sex Discrimination Act is mainly concerned with discrimination against individuals and to a lesser extent against groups of workers. It doesn't concern itself with the structure of industry – with the hours and conditions offered in certain kinds of work. It does have sections which cover education and training, but the individual cases which have been brought about, for example, girls' right to study metalwork, have done little to change the structure of the education system either – there have been no great moves to encourage girls in general to study metalwork as opposed to giving certain individual girls this choice.

How would you set about changing the structure of work to give women a fairer chance? Can the Sex Discrimination Act be of any use? These are big questions, and ones which have not been answered in terms of trade union policy for most unions. It's worth finding out whether your union has any policies about ways to improve women's conditions at work. If you don't think your union has a strong enough policy, it's up to you to change it – check your rule book to see how policies are made in your own union. You can get further help from another book in this series, *Getting Organized*.

Before we leave the Equal Pay and Sex Discrimination Acts, we should take a quick look at the Equal Opportunities Commission (EOC), the body set up to keep an eye on these laws and the position of women generally. The EOC gives advice, produces numerous reports, and can sometimes give legal aid. It is made up of representatives nominated by the Secretary of State, including TUC and CBI members. The EOC can also deal with complaints about discriminatory job adverts and serve non discrimination notices on people or companies not observing either Act. These notices are the first step to taking court action to get information and make sure that the Acts are not broken again.

You can find out more about the EOC by reading the full guide to the Sex Discrimination Act which you can get free – along with other EOC publications – from the EOC at Overseas House, Quay Street, Manchester M3 3HN. tel: 061 833 9244.

## Part-time workers' rights

In recent years Parliament has stepped further into the area of workers' rights and made changes to the old legal rights which were based simply on the rights of master and servant under the contract of employment. Redundancy and unfair dismissal have been the main focus of changes in individual rights. Legal rights that workers have gained under, for example, the Trade Union and Labour Relations Act and the Employment Protection Act can, however, be claimed only under certain conditions – most importantly, having given a period of service to the same employer, and working more than a certain number of hours per week. A ministerial order in 1979 increased the required period of service from twenty-six to fifty-two weeks – which means that workers dismissed for no reason at all will have no right to take their employer to a Tribunal unless they have been employed for fifty-two weeks.

More important from the point of view of women workers is the hours per week requirement. Since the Employment Protection Act of 1975 this has been sixteen hours a week (a change from the twenty-one hours per week originally required) with people who have worked more than eight hours

per week for five years also qualifying. What do you think
of these requirements? Is it fair to give the same rights to
someone who works sixteen hours per week as to someone
who works forty or more? Should people who work between
eight and sixteen hours per week have to wait five years
before being able to make a complaint to a tribunal if their
employer suddenly turns round and fires them for no reason
at all?

One obvious conclusion to draw from the limitations the
law puts on who can go to a tribunal is that we should rely
on union organization rather than the law to protect us from
employers behaving unreasonably. But lots of women are in
part-time work in small, un-unionized places – small shops,
cafes, and offices, and as cleaners for small firms. For these
women, at the moment, the law is their only protection. For
many other women the law forms a basis for union agreements – a set of minimum standards.

One other point to bear in mind about part-time workers
is that employers can often out manoeuvre legal changes. In
1975, many school cleaners in Aberdeen, like those in many
other cities, had their hours cut from twenty per week to
fifteen as part of the Labour Government's cuts. In 1980,
school dinner ladies in the same city were being asked to
agree to a reduction in weekly hours from ten to fourteen to
seven and a half, as part of the Conservative Government's
cuts. In both cases, as well as losing hours these workers
stood to lose their entitlement to legal rights. A cynic might
also remark that in the case of school cleaners it is interesting
that pre-1975 their hours per week were one hour less than
the minimum to qualify for full-time workers legal rights and
later school meals hours changed – once again to one hour
less than the part-time minimum.

We have already looked at maternity rights in Chapter two
and you will remember that the same qualifications about
hours per week applies to these too. Small employers were
also let off the hook by the Employment Act on women's
right to return after maternity leave.

# Equal rights at work?

Do you think the problems faced by women at work *have* been solved by the laws which have come in during the seventies? Will they work, given more time? If not, what are the real problems and how do we tackle them? What do we need to do in terms of trade union organization and trade union policy? Let's wind up this chapter with a summary of some of the problems and the bits of law that have tried to solve them.

**Low pay for women**  The Equal Pay Act 1970 tried to introduce equal pay for equal work – plus equal pay for jobs given the same value on a job evaluation scheme. This is not a broad enough change – we need the right to 'equal pay for work of equal value' before we can begin to challenge the low value given to women's work.

**Poor opportunites for women to move into male jobs or get promoted**  The Sex Discrimination Act 1975 gave the legal right not to be discriminated against on grounds of sex or marriage. Discrimination is difficult to prove, especially without information from employers. In any case, past educational and work experience still tend to lead to women and girls ending up in women's work and family responsibilities encourage women to look for part-time work – almost always 'women's work' and badly paid.

**Poor job security for part-time workers**  The Trade Union and Labour Relations Act gave certain rights to those working over twenty-one hours per week. The Employment Protection Act gives rights to those working over sixteen hours per week and to those with five years service who do eight hours a week or more. What a long time to wait for rights! And what about people who work less than eight hours for one employer?

**Poor job security for pregnant women and mothers with young children**  The Employment Protection Act 1975 included the right not to be dismissed for pregnancy, to get maternity pay and to be able to return to your job if you worked the right hours and had enough service. The maternity rights are not as good as they could be, and a lack of childcare facilities makes keeping on a job much harder for anyone with responsibility for children.

The law hasn't solved these problems. What are we going to do as trade unionists and what has already been achieved by trade unions? We will be looking at this in the last three chapters.

# Further reading

The Equal Opportunities Commission (their address is at the end of Chapter two) produces information on the areas we have looked at in this chapter. Write for a list of their reports on, for example, employers' policies and practices on equal opportunities in employment, or protective legislation. They also supply free guides to the Equal Pay and Sex Discrimination Acts – ask for the full guides, not the short leaflets if you want a reasonable amount of detail.

*The Equality Report* Jean Coussins, (NCCL, 1976) describes the way the Equal Pay and Sex Discrimination Acts did – or didn't – work in practice in their first year. *The Equal Pay and Sex Discrimination Acts – Report from Scotland*, Margaret Marshall and Chris Aldred (Aberdeen People's Press, 1977) does the same job from a Scottish point of view.

The NCCL Rights for Women Unit has more to offer to follow up specific problems mentioned in this chapter. *Women Factory Workers – the case against repealing the protective laws*, Anna Coote (NCCL, 1975) gives one point of view on a problem we have looked at. *Part-time workers need full-time rights*, Ann Sedley (NCCL, 1980) and *Gay Workers: Trade Unions and the Law*, Chris Beer, Roland Jeffery, and Terry Munyard (NCCL, 1981) give you more detail on two other areas.

*Womens Rights*, Anna Coote and Tess Gill (Penguin, 1977) and *Scottish Woman's Place*, Eveline Hunter (EUSPB, 1978) are both practical handbooks on women's rights – not just at work. At least one of them should be on your bookshelf for reference, or get your union branch to buy a copy.

*Health and Safety at Work*, Dave Eva and Ron Oswald (Pan, 1981) goes into more detail on health and safety than we have had room for here.

Incomes Data Services produce regular publications on all aspects of legal rights for workers, and on collective agreements. From time to time they also produce excellent handbooks on, for example, equal pay, giving up-to-date developments. It's all pretty detailed, and not the kind of thing you would want to read for fun. But if it's up-to-date detail you want, go along to your local reference or commercial library – they should be able to show you a selection of recent IDS material.

# Chapter **Four**

## Women and trade union organization

In the first three chapters of this book we have looked at the kinds of work women do, how domestic responsibilities fit in with women's working lives and how the law affects women at work. Hopefully you were thinking, 'Why don't women do something about this?' or 'How can I change this through my union?' as you read the earlier chapters. In this half of the book we will be looking at what can be done to change the situation. Let's split the problems into two kinds, and look at each in turn.

● How can trade unions organize and represent women

better? In particular, how can we get more women to join the unions, and how can we make sure union rules and procedures give women a real say?

 How can trade unions encourage more participation and activism by women?

In this chapter we will be looking at organization and representation, and at the problems faced by unions and by women members in these areas. The problem of participation is a deeper one, and we will look at that in the next chapter.

## How can trade unions organize and represent women better?

Have you ever heard a trade union official say 'Women are such a problem to organize'? Would you agree? And if you do agree, why do you think this is? Does the problem spring from practical difficulties or from people's attitudes? What sort of difficulties can you think of for a union which wants to encourage more women to join? What sort of problems can you foresee for a union in giving the best possible representation to women members? Let's look at these questions in a bit more detail.

### Recruitment of women

No one could deny that in many situations there *are* practical problems in recruiting women. You will remember that women tend to work in smaller workplaces, and in less skilled jobs than men. Practically all part-time workers are women. Each of these facts causes problems.

**Small workplaces**   It's much harder to organize people in small firms for several reasons – let's try and list a few.

● Small firms can be more personal – workers may regard the employer as a personal friend and may even see the firm's well-being as identical with their own. An active

93

union in this situation can feel like 'ganging up' on the boss. People's actual jobs and rates of pay may be more individualized too – and that helps to undermine solidarity with other workers.

● In a larger company you are almost certain to find two or three people who are keen on the union and who can tell you what is going on at branch meetings and so on. You will probably see someone you recognize from work at a branch meeting, so it won't all seem so strange to you at your first meeting. If you work in a small place, the chances are not so good that one of your workmates will keep you in touch with the union, or that you will recognize someone at a branch meeting.

● Union branches often seem to be mostly concerned with the issues that are important to members working for the larger employers – obviously, as that is probably where most members are, but if you work for a small firm you may well feel you are being ignored.

● Lots of large firms operate a check-off system – deducting union subs from wages. If there's no check-off there may be a union collector. Either way, it's a good deal easier to remember to pay your dues than if you have to go to the union office or branch meeting to pay them. No wonder people in small workplaces often fall into arrears and let their trade union membership lapse unless there is an energetic official who makes sure they don't.

● What can a union really achieve in a small workplace? Obviously the first thing a union will try to do will be to improve pay and conditions through agreements with the employer. But there is far less scope in a small firm for some of the more exciting developments in collective bargaining (making agreements between union and employer). In big workplaces unions can catch members' imaginations with information about company profits, or multinational connections – in a small firm everyone probably has an idea how good business is from the gossip; who needs an agreement that management will disclose information to the union? There's much less chance for a display of fireworks from the union by revealing, for example, that company profits are at an all-time high despite their reluctance to pay up on the wage claim. Obviously this doesn't matter most of the time – but it can mean a rather low-profile union.

All these problems affect men and women alike. But as more women work in smaller firms the problems are that much more important for women.

**Less skilled work**   Another thing you will remember about women's work is that women often do less skilled jobs than men. We have already talked about the way unions have fought to retain skilled status for jobs through only allowing union members access to certain jobs and imposing a condition that these workers are fully trained. All that depends on the job itself, or other jobs related to it, having at least at one time required a real skill which was in great demand by employers; and maintenance of skilled status still depends on some shortage of suitable labour. Skilled status *does* mean extra bargaining power – and few women work in the jobs which bring this extra power. Rising unemployment creates special difficulty for the unskilled – and this is going to be the major problem of the 1980s.

**Part-time work**   There is a vast army of women part-time workers, doing all kinds of different jobs, and in most cases taking lower wages and worse conditions than a full-timer would put up with. The ideal solution to combining earning some money with domestic responsibilities is to a lot of women to take a part-time job, and this results in lots of people chasing too few jobs. Women are well aware that they are 'lucky' to get a part-time job, and employers are not slow to use this to keep their employees from making too much of a fuss. What problems will this lead to in trying to recruit part-timers to trade unions? Remember too that legal rights are worth little to people who work short hours or who take on work on a casual basis. Let's list some of the problems.

● If you take home a small wage, you are less likely to want

95

to spend much on a union subscription. (Many unions do, however, offer a lower rate for part-time workers.)

● If you are only at work for part of the day it is a bit easier to put up with a bad deal when you are there – especially when you know there are heaps of others who would love your job, and when you have little legal protection if your employer sacks you.

● Even if you do part-time work in a big workplace, you may not be there at the same time as most of the union activists – for example if you clean a big office, or work on the twilight shift at a factory.

● Many part-timers are married women (70 per cent of them in fact). Many of these women will have families to look after, and for many it may be their first job after being at home for a few years with children. It may be years since they were in a union and like many women returning to work they may have little confidence. Neither of these things is likely to make them want to join the union.

**Jobs caring for people** A large proportion of women workers do jobs that involve caring for other people, either directly, like nurses and teachers, or indirectly, like workers in hospital laundries or the school meals service. Traditional forms of trade union action do not often appeal to these workers, who don't want to bring about unnecessary suffering for those uninvolved in the union's dispute. A reluctance to be involved in strikes which might 'hurt the patient', for example, can lead to a reluctance to join the union. Many unions in the public sector have begun to take account of this, and are developing new forms of industrial action to attempt to deal with this problem.

We have reviewed four problem areas for union recruitment – small employers, less skilled work, part-time work, and jobs caring for people. And yet, women *are* joining unions, and in large numbers, too. At least we are partly on the way towards getting women workers into trade unions, but this still leaves us the big question of how the unions can best *represent* women, and build up genuine organization on a stronger basis than just being able to count up a large membership on paper. Once in a union, what do women want from it?

## Why have women been joining unions?

Why does anyone join a trade union? Perhaps to get a job in a workplace where there is a closed shop. Perhaps to reassure themselves that they will get legal help if they have an accident at work, of if they are blamed for a costly mistake at work. Perhaps to have someone who will stand up for them if they get into trouble. Perhaps because they want to get better pay. Perhaps because a workmate nags them into it. Or even, perhaps, because they want to take advantage of the union's discount scheme or cheap holidays. Some people join because they believe in trade unions as a way of improving life for working people. Whatever the reason, though, most people join a union at least partly because they think it will help them in some way.

So are there any particular reasons why women join trade unions? Or any particular reasons why women workers are still less likely to be in a union than men? Do women have the same reasons for joining unions as men have? What do women want from trade unions? What kind of effort are women prepared to put into trade unions? Sometimes looking back over the years can help to answer this kind of question.

Let's look at how things have been changing since the Second World War. Lots of women had been encouraged to go out to work during the war, the men were away soldiering and so trade union membership in wartime included a larger proportion than usual of women (about 20 per cent). At the end of the war many women left their paid work and returned to the home, and women's numbers in the trade unions fell back to about 15 per cent of the total membership – roughly the same level as the pre-war figures.

## The fifties

In the late forties, married women began to go back out to paid work. There were less single women both in the population as a whole and in the work-force, and in the fifties around a million married women joined the work-force. By the end of the fifties for the first time, a woman going out to work was just as likely to be married as to be single. (In 1951 44 per cent of women going out to work were married – in 1959 this figure had reached 53 per cent. But these figures don't take into account all the married women who were actually *earning* – by taking in homework, doing cleaning or childminding – jobs which were usually unregistered, and so didn't get into the statistics.)

The growth in the numbers of women out at work, as a result of more married women joining the work-force did not immediately produce a dramatic increase in women's trade union membership. Throughout the fifties only about one working woman in four was a trade union member, compared to about one working man in two. Everyone blamed this on apathy and lack of trade union consciousness in women except for a few activists who recognized the different situation of most women at work – both in terms of the jobs they did and of their responsibilities in the home – and saw that trade unions in general, whatever they *said*, were not *doing* much for women

In the fifties the main trade union problems for women were – as usual – low pay (and the resulting need for equal pay), restricted access to jobs and trade union rights and the difficulties of fitting in domestic tasks, particularly childcare, with paid work. Progress in all these areas was, to say the least, disappointing, although as a result of members' action, equal pay was won for some workers in the public services and some unions began to challenge promotion structures which resulted in inexperienced young men being promoted in preference to more experienced women with longer service. But in 1952, the TSSA (Transport Salaried Staffs Association) at conference still decided *not* to support women's rights even to *apply* for some posts and many trade unions were still excluding women from doing certain jobs, having returned to pre-war restrictive practices which had been lifted during wartime giving women a wider range of job opportunities.

Some unions tried to win the interest of women members by columns for women in their journals. The columns included fashion and beauty hints and recipes and in 1959 the TUC Women's Advisory Committee announced a new 'feminine' recruitment campaign – fashion shows where women could be persuaded to join the unions too. Yet at the same time as going to these lengths to attact women members, many trade unions were ignoring a rather more direct appeal to women – fighting for real improvements for women members. Despite commitments on paper to equal pay, many unions continued to settle for wage rises which in fact *increased* differentials between men and women – a trend which continued through the sixties.

## The sixties

In the sixties even more married women went out to work, and by the end of the sixties three out of five women out at work were married. The sixties were the real take-off point for the growth of women's membership of the unions. While the number of men in TUC-affiliated unions remained pretty steady, women's membership grew half as big again, and by the end of the decade one in five TUC-affiliated trade unionists were women. This growth rate is slightly misleading, as during the 1960s two unions with a large number of female members joined the TUC – the NUT (National Union of Teachers) and NALGO (The National and Local Goverment Officers' Association). But even without these two unions joining the TUC there was an increase in women trade union members – and, over the decade, in women's militancy.

Equal pay was perhaps *the* issue of the sixties. Non-manual workers in the public services had got equal pay by 1961 and were pushing for a whole range of demands – maternity leave, equal opportunities, equal terms and conditions. But these women were doing better than most. Nineteen unions (representing 200,000 women) replied to a TUC survey in 1962 that they had equal pay agreements – a good number of these for public employees. But a further thirty unions had no such agreements.

In 1963, the TUC conference carried a motion calling on the next Labour government (which in fact came to power the next year) to legislate for equal pay. The Women's Advisory Committee of the TUC put forward a charter, the 'Industrial Charter for Women', in 1963, demanding equal pay, equal opportunities for training, retraining facilities for women returning to industry, and special provisions for the health and welfare of women at work – still fairly limited demands, but a start. By 1966, things still didn't seem to be happening on equal pay and at conference that year the TUC were attacked for their half-hearted action to date – which had included a meeting with a government Minister *at which no women had been present*.

The mood of women had changed since the 1950s – the idea that women should be full-time mothers so that their children grew up 'normal' was losing popularity as more and more women were able to get jobs as a result of labour shortages and took the opportuntity to go out to work. And the big increases in women's numbers within the unions did a great deal to boost women's confidence, forcing men to take them and their interests more seriously.

As well as beginning to express clearly and formally dissatisfaction with the efforts of the trade union leadership on equal pay and other issues of vital importance to women, female delegates to the TUC and its Women's Advisory Committee began to question the old argument that women just weren't interested in trade unions. The 1967 report of the Women's Advisory Committee drew attention to the fact that although women's numbers in unions had been increasing at a slightly faster rate than men's numbers, there was still one male trade unionist for every two male workers and one female trade unionist for every four female workers. For the first time the report said this was *not* the fault of women workers themselves, but reflected instead the kinds of jobs done by women. Where women worked in the same jobs as men and the men were well-organized, so were the women.

The same report pointed out examples where the unions themselves were at fault. Few unions had women officials, especially at executive level. Many unions restricted women to special sections with smaller dues – and restricted benefits. Years later, at the end of the seventies, UCATT, the construction union, had to change its rules, as it still had no membership category into which it could accept skilled women.

The report also recognised the importance of domestic resposibilities, and that men were going to have to use their trade union strength to help women's organization and fight for women's demands.

The changes in attitude of the Women's Advisory Committee reflected a growth of militancy among many women trade unionists. Women members had begun to demand that their unions did not ignore policies on equal pay by continuing to increase differentials between men's and women's rates when negotiating wage agreements. Unions who claimed women should 'let their union know what they want' were reminded sharply that there were already agreed policies on equal pay, and some unions began to accept the need to give higher value to women's skills. The engineering union began to close up the differences between men's and women's pay – although John Boyd at the 1965 women's conference of that union was quite capable of proudly announcing the gains for women and still saying 'I never want the women of this country to lose their femininity' and explaining he would not like to see women doing hard, heavy, dirty and hazardous jobs. Would it be unkind to ask if he meant he hoped women would stay in traditional 'women's work' and that 'men's work' should still be protected from an influx of female labour?

Women began to take more industrial action for equal pay, culminating in the famous 1968 strike among sewing machinists at Ford's Dagenham plant. Recognition of the women's skill was demanded, along with parity with men in the C grade. They settled for 92 per cent of this rate, but Rose

101

Boland of the strike committee was probably right when she said, 'I think the Ford women have definitely shaken the country.' The women had organized their own strike committee with official union backing, had brought Ford to a standstill, and had created enough of a stir to bring in Barbara Castle, then Secretary of State for Employment, to help get a settlement.

The Ford strike acted as a focus for women's dissatisfaction with the slow progress of the trade union leadership, and as a terrific boost for the confidence of working women at local level. The interest aroused by the strike also came at a time when the women's liberation movement was getting off the ground – and feminist ideas sharpened criticism of the deal women were getting from the unions. Demands for legislation on equal pay and equal opportunities were made both at TUC Conference and a special TUC conference on equal pay in 1968. The TUC's Annual Report had once again indicated lack of progress, and referred to economic circumstances as an excuse for lack of government action.

NJACCWER – the National Joint Action Campaign Committee for Women's Equal Rights – had come into existence as a result of the Ford strike, and began to organize an equal pay demonstration, which took place in May 1969, and was supported by women trade unionists from all over the country. Trade unions seized the chance provided by this upsurge of interest to launch recruiting campaigns based on promises of fighting for equal pay. The Government began to draft an equal pay bill and responses were required from trade unions and the TUC. Action seemed to be on the way and the period of rapid growth of trade unionism among women workers had begun.

## The seventies

The seventies saw the introduction of the Equal Pay Act in 1970 and its full implementation, along with the Sex Discrimination Act, in December 1975. The late sixties and early seventies also saw more growth in the numbers of women in employment, particularly of married women out at work

– by the late 1970s married women outnumbered single women in the work-force by more than two to one.

The last couple of years of the sixties were the start of the great boom in the recruitment of women to trade unions; this boom continued through the seventies. A pamphlet called 'Women, Work and Trade Union Organization' by Judith Hunt and Shelley Adams, available from the WEA, gives a lot more detail on this, but here are a few examples.

● NUPE (The National Union of Public Employees) which represents, among others, some council workers, hospital workers, and university and college clerical staff and manual workers, more than trebled its female membership between 1968 and 1978.

● NALGO (The National and Local Government Officers' Association) which represents clerical and administrative workers in a wide range of public services had well over double as many women members in 1978 compared to 1968.

● COHSE (The Confederation of Health Service Employees), which represents health service workers, had an even larger increase (as a proportion of its size) in the number of women members, with more than four times the number of women members in 1978 than there were in 1968.

● ASTMS (The Association of Scientific, Technical and Managerial Staffs), organizing workers in various types of administrative, clerical, scientific and technical jobs showed a seven times greater number of women members in 1978 than 1968.

The reasons for increases in female membership are quite complex. It's not just that the unions have been dashing out to recruit women, or that more women are now in the jobs traditionally organized by a particular union. Some unions have always tended to recruit men, others women. The National Union of Tailor and Garment Workers has always been a 'woman's union' – 92 per cent of its members were women in 1980. The National Union of Teachers is two-thirds women, when the NUT joined the TUC in 1970 it brought in 200,000 women members. The concentration of women in these unions says more about the kind of jobs represented than about the union's recruitment strategies or policies.

Other women tend to be members of the larger general unions, particularly those which organize public sector workers, rather than the smaller craft unions which have tradionally organized skilled workers. NUPE and COHSE are just two examples of general unions which have greatly increased their membership by recruitment of women in the public sector. Many areas of 'women's work' have proved to be good areas for unions on the look-out for new members; traditionally these have been areas of poor trade union organization. There are two ways to describe where the increase in trade union membership in the 1970s has come from. Looked at one way, the increase has been among women trade unionists – from another angle, the increase is among white-collar workers. Both the influx of women and of white-collar trade unionists has begun to point to the end of the old stereotype of 'a trade unionist' – the skilled male manual worker.

We have looked at the overall picture of women's recruitment to the trade unions since the late 1950s. But the overall picture doesn't really tell us why individual women joined unions. It's all very well to describe the kinds of jobs the new recruits do, or to say which unions were most sucessful in attracting new members, but it doesn't really explain why more women came to think it was worth joining the union. We must know these reasons – both so that we know how to attract women into membership, and so that we know how to represent their interests. Why *did* women join the unions? What do women expect from the unions? Here are some of the possibilities; you will probably be able to think of more.

● Women joined unions in large numbers in the seventies because more women went out to work in the sixties and it took a few years to get trade union ideas across to these new recruits to the work-force.

● In the sixties, despite lip service to equal pay, trade unions had achieved little until the Ford strike and growing militancy began to force union action. Once unions began to take action which was clearly in the interests of women trade union members, women began to see the point of joining unions.

● The idea that mothers should not go out to work had taken a few hard knocks when mothers began to go to work in large numbers without their children suffering noticeably. Once this idea was out of the way, women began to take their paid work more seriously and to want better pay and conditions at work, rather than feeling guilty for being out at work at all.

● The large number of married women out at work meant that families began to look on a woman's 'second wage' as an important contribution to the family's standard of living rather than as 'pin money'. As soon as a woman's wage became a necessity rather than a luxury, that wage seemed worth fighting for, and the trade unions seemed the appropriate place for that fight.

● Separation and divorce became much more common in the 1970s, with, for example, one in three Scottish marriages ending in divorce (remember divorce is still – in 1981 – more difficult in Scotland than in England and Wales). Perhaps women began to see the need to be able to support themselves in case the male breadwinner disappeared – and the new importance this gave to keeping paid work and getting a good wage helped trade unionism to develop more rapidly among women.

● The trade unions began to recognize that the influx of women on to the labour market must be unionized – or threaten trade unionists everywhere with cheap labour. Recruitment campaigns began to work because unions genuinely *wanted* women recruits now.

● Unions were competing for recruits in a time of intense competition between trade unions for bargaining rights. The fastest way to increase membership was to recruit women.

● Legal changes began to give women confidence that there

were rights to be claimed, and that women's conditions at work – and perhaps outside work too – *could* and *should* be changed.

● Feminist ideas began to be taken a bit more seriously by the television, radio and newspapers, and although lots of people still began their remarks with the words 'I'm not a Women's Libber, but . . .' it began to be more acceptable to argue that women got a bad deal in relation to men.

● The introduction of equal pay gave women a big fright. If employers were going to have to pay women the same as men perhaps they just wouldn't employ women . . . Trade unions seemed the only way to defend jobs.

Probably none of these things caused the upsurge in recruitment on their own. But each possibility does reflect one or more of the changes in women's roles which were happening at the same time. Which items in the list above would you be inclined to write off as irrelevant in the light of your own experience? Which do you think ring true?

If you are a women and joined a union for the first time in the late sixties or early seventies, what made *you* join? What about the other women who joined at the same time? If you were already in a union, did your union get a lot of new recruits who were women? Why did they join? If there were very few women in your union in the sixties and there are still very few now, why is this?

It is perhaps an impossible task for any one of us to try and make sense of all this on our own, without the benefit of each other's experiences. As trade unionists should we be trying to make sense of this bit of recent trade union history by discussion in our union branches, at our workplaces, and at local trades councils? Should these questions receive special consideration from women's committees or equal opportunities groups within the trade union movement? Do we need to look outside the trade union movement for answers? Is it important to try to work out why women joined the unions, or should we just be getting on with trying to get a good deal for women at work now? Have women got what they wanted from the unions? Will women leave the unions again, and if so, what will make women go? Will women change the way trade unions do things?

## Union response to growth in female membership

Trade unions have been changing right through this century, with the most marked recent change being the growth of the shop-steward's movement. Does the growth in women's membership require another big change in direction or organization from the trade unions? The Women's TUC Report for 1978–9 said:

'Some trade unions have not yet appreciated that . . . the remarkable and rapid increase in women's membership of unions is more revolutionary than evolutionary, and that as such it requires a new approach.'

We can't get an easy answer by looking at what other countries have done either. The same report tells us that only in the Scandinavian unions will we find as high a proportion of women as we have in Britain. As the Scandanavian countries have much smaller populations than Britain, this still means we in Britain have the largest number of women trade unionists of all the countries with which we have international links.

Do you think, as the report says, that unions will eventually have to accept that the increases in women's numbers within the unions *does* require a revolutionary change in the way the trade unions look at things? Is the change, as they say, revolutionary rather than evolutionary? In other words, is the growth in women's membership something different for the unions, or really just more of the same? Do the growing unions simply have to deal with a fairly large new membership with a lack of experience – or must the unions do something special to take account of the fact that many of the new members are women?

*Accommodating the new women members – changes in trade unionism*

What do you think are the main problems which faced the trade unions as a result of women joining the unions in large numbers? What sort of changes were forced on the unions, and what other changes might have benefited the trade union interests of the new women members?

Let's look first at the problems and try to make a list:

- An influx of inexperienced members.
- A need to deal with new industries, or new jobs, which the union may not know much about.
- A lot of new members whose interest in the union came in for a lot of suspicious and potentially divisive remarks from existing members.
- Lots of new members with heavy domestic commitments.
- New members pushing for a number of quite specific – and quite major – changes at work and in social services and benefits, everything from equal pay to maternity leave, improved childcare, and an end to sex discrimination at work.

How did the unions respond, if at all? First, they mostly threw their weight behind the campaign for *laws* to improve women's position at work; these campaigns were in fact quite successful. But why did the trade unions decide to go for *legal* changes rather than trying to improve conditions by bargaining with employers? Trade unionists had always mistrusted the law – why did they go for action through Parliament and new laws in this case? Did something push the unions into tangling with the law? Here are a few suggestions – you may be able to think of others:

- Recognition that many women worked for small employers and that this made large-scale campaigns to reach agreements with all employers impracticable.
- A lack of faith that there would in fact be widespread support for action to achieve collective agreements of this kind, and consequently a fear to risk failure in negotiations through lack of membership support.

- Fear that employers would demand concessions on other issues (perhaps more important issues for some of the membership) in return for granting some of the women's demands in agreements.
- Unwillingness to recognize that equal pay and other improvements in women's conditions were really trade union matters.
- Genuine lack of membership support, although union leaders were convinced of the need for equal pay.
- Unwillingness to bargain on issues which could be divisive of the membership.
- A desire to protect weakly organized workers as well as those with good trade union organization.
- The belief that changes in law would change social attitudes faster than changes in agreements.
- Mistrust that women would take industrial action if it became necessary.

Whatever the reasons, does the attempt to change the law amount to an acceptance that bargaining would not have been successful?

Why did the unions have so little faith in their ability to win improvements for women members? Of course, motions recommending action through collective bargaining on, for example, equal pay had been passed for years, and nothing much had happened. Was the resort to the law just acceptance of the realities? And why did the unions decide to go ahead with limited membership support rather than throwing all their efforts into organizing women effectively so that collective bargaining *would* work? Of course that is a longer-term strategy, taking longer to show results. Did unions prefer easier and quicker gains through Parliament rather than long term changes in organization eventually leading to improvements through bargaining for women?

That takes us back again to our original question about the trade union response to the influx of women members. How hard would it have been to organize the women effectively to improve conditions? Let's concentrate on the practical problems first – here are two big ones:

- inexperience of new members and resulting lack of confidence in organizing and taking action;
- domestic responsibilities interfering with trade union activities.

The first problem – inexperience – is not unique to new women members, and is really a problem for trade union education. Trade union education, particularly through the TUC scheme for training representatives, did expand during the late sixties and seventies – but the TUC Education Department has reported a disappointingly low take-up of these courses by women. We will need to look at this problem again later, and will do so in Chapter six, but for the moment let's go on to look at domestic responsibilities.

In Chapter two we looked at the way having domestic responsibilities as well as a paid job affects women at work. The same responsibilities may get in the way of trade union involvement. How can we make trade union involvement easier for both men and women with responsibilities at home?

The TUC charter on equality for women, which is reprinted in full in Chapter six suggests that times of meetings and the availability of childcare will be the key points for deciding whether or not women will attend trade union events in reasonable numbers. The charter recommends:

- branch meetings during working hours where possible, and better still, with no loss of pay;
- childcare facilities for use by any adult responsible for children, arranged in connection with trade union meetings at all levels.

Let's examine these ideas in more detail. When might they work, and when are they totally impractical? Does your union already do any of these things? If so, do they work? If not, why not?

Branch meetings during working hours, particularly if no one loses any pay, are an obvious advantage to all members. People who have had to organize childcare to get to work at all will also benefit by not having to make arrangements to get out again to the union meeting. Obviously this won't work where the branch members come from a variety of different workplaces, especially if the workplaces are a fair distance apart or if even a few members can't get the time off. Lunchtime meetings may be a compromise, but once again women are often off organizing the domestic side of their responsibilities getting shopping, meeting children from school, making a meal for the family, or whatever. Loss of pay will also be a key issue, and we tend to get stuck with a bit of a 'Catch 22' situation – if the union was better organized, paid time off for union meetings would be easier to negotiate; if there was paid time off, the union could get better organized.

If workplace branches are not a possibility and meetings without loss of pay during working hours can't be sorted out, childcare of some kind becomes essential. In any case, once you get above branch level, meetings will begin to need childcare arrangements anyway – parents and other adults who look after children may have to travel some distance, or attend at weekends or during the evenings, and the childcare arrangements they usually make to go to work often just won't cover the necessary times.

What sort of childcare might be needed? Everyone probably now thinks of a crèche at the meeting as the simplest solution, but this may not be the best answer. Babysitting rotas may be a better idea, and older children may need quite different arrangements.

But one thing is always true; if the childcare is rotten, the adults won't come back very often. If your child bursts into tears as soon as she or he hears she or he is going to a crèche, the whole performance of getting to the meeting is that much more difficult – and it's that much more likely you won't bother next time. It's always an effort to cart children about on public transport, especially if they are young and can't get on and off buses alone. If they are miserable, it's even worse. The apathy of working mothers is a bit easier to understand when you realize the effort of getting a child ready, getting to the meeting, finding the place where the child is to be looked after, settling in the child, going to the meeting, picking up the child, getting the child ready and going home. If going to the meeting is interrupted by an unhappy child, or if the mother is called to the crèche, will any parent be likely to think it's worth all the effort?

If there's no crèche it will be worse – just add on the journey to and from the childminders assuming you have managed to find someone to look after your child, and that you can afford to pay them if necessary (or that you have the time to return the favour for *their* children). Crèches during the evening aren't very satisfactory anyway for pre-school children. Bedtime may come slap bang in the middle of the agenda and if the child stays up she or he may be difficult tomorrow. If the child goes to sleep she or he will probably wake up on the way home and keep you up for hours when you get there.

What would you need to do to arrange childcare at your meetings? The crèche can be a disaster unless someone has bothered to take the time to organize it properly. You will need:

● enough space, preferably in a separate room;
● toys suitable for the right age group;
● someone who can think of things the children will enjoy doing and who can cope in emergencies;
● enough other adults or older children to take young ones to the toilet, play with the children, and take over in an emergency.

This may seem like a lot to ask, but bitter experience shows that bad childcare can soon lead to no one using it – its all too easy to then say: 'We tried providing childcare but there was no demand.'

Babysitting may be a better answer, but you have to find people to do it – not always easy – and parents may feel guilty about using a babysitting service unless it's really important that they go to the meeting rather than just finding out about it at work tomorrow.

Conferences and meetings away from home are even trickier. You may find the crèche runs for exactly the same hours as the formal sessions and you are expected to pick up your children at breaks and mealtimes and attend to them yourself – which doesn't exactly help your concentration or help you to meet and talk to your fellow trade unionists.

All this makes childcare sound a terrible problem. It *is* difficult at the moment, mostly because we are still pretty inexperienced at arranging suitable childcare and because we don't think about childcare first or regard childcare as a priority when we are deciding on time and place of meetings and so on. Where there's a will there's a way . . . Unions should be working on producing suitable advice and handbooks on childcare if we really think it is important to organize women. Perhaps unions also ought to provide cash to pay for childcare too as an ordinary benefit for members attending meetings. What do you think? Are these practical suggestions? Can we afford to ignore the problem?

## Effective representation of women

There are a couple of points we mentioned earlier still outstanding – trade union inexperience in dealing with industries employing women and in dealing with women's employers, and suspicion of new women members from existing trade union members.

In order to negotiate well on behalf of members, trade union representatives have to have quite detailed knowledge of the types of jobs members do, and of the sorts of problems the members feel are important. It is common trade union practice to involve members or stewards from a particular department when working conditions there are being discussed, even though the factory convenor or full-time union official involved may have a pretty good idea of what things are like him- or herself. This is just good sense – no one understands what conditions are really like as well as the person who works under them.

Let's take a bit of a detour back. Remember women and men tend to do different jobs. Now look at Figure 4.

You will see from it that *no* union in that list has as many women executive members, full-time officials or TUC delegates as you would expect from the proportion of women in

113

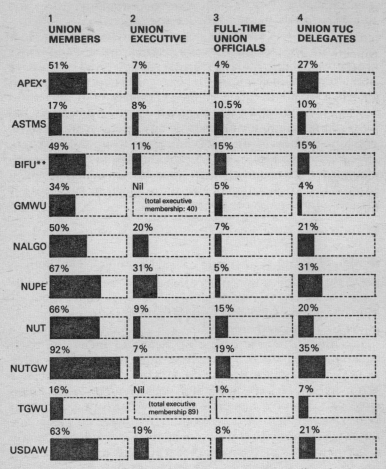

| | 1 UNION MEMBERS | 2 UNION EXECUTIVE | 3 FULL-TIME UNION OFFICIALS | 4 UNION TUC DELEGATES |
|---|---|---|---|---|
| APEX* | 51% | 7% | 4% | 27% |
| ASTMS | 17% | 8% | 10.5% | 10% |
| BIFU** | 49% | 11% | 15% | 15% |
| GMWU | 34% | Nil (total executive membership: 40) | 5% | 4% |
| NALGO | 50% | 20% | 7% | 21% |
| NUPE | 67% | 31% | 5% | 31% |
| NUT | 66% | 9% | 15% | 20% |
| NUTGW | 92% | 7% | 19% | 35% |
| TGWU | 16% | Nil (total executive membership 89) | 1% | 7% |
| USDAW | 63% | 19% | 8% | 21% |

\* Association of Professional, Executive, Clerical and Computer Staffs.
\*\* Banking, Insurance and Finance Union.

*Figure 4* Women in union jobs

The shaded area in each column represents the percentage of women present in each of the four groups shown: 1. total union membership; 2. the unions' national executives; 3. full-time officials of that union; and 4. TUC delegates of that union.

the membership. The ten unions listed account for two-thirds of all women in trade unions – so they are not just exceptional examples. It's a pity that figures for shop-stewards are not often available; most unions say that a greater number of women are now coming forward as workplace representatives than in the past, and that there are more women at shop-steward level than in the higher status positions we have looked at.

What does this mean at the workplace, and for the ordinary trade union member? On average, her shop-steward may be a woman, but as we have seen, it's likely her union full-time officer will be a man, her representative on the unions national executive will be a man, and the representatives her union sends to the TUC will mostly be men. We have noted three things;

● Union representation is often at it's best when backed up by personal experience.
● Men and women are likely to do different jobs, and to have different problems in trying to combine work and home life.
● Women are frequently represented by men.

Can these three things tell us anything about the quality of union representation for women? Not necessarily that women won't be well represented, but perhaps that unless male representatives take the trouble to really find out what 'women's work' is like on a day to day basis, *and* to look thoroughly at any problems at work which arise from the ever-present second job at home, they won't be good representatives. This isn't a new idea – lots of unions have for years given preference, when choosing full-time officials, to people with working experience in the particular trade; and officials without this background have been strongly encouraged to learn about the practical aspects of their members' work.

Have unions been encouraging officials to learn enough about women's jobs? Does any trade union regard it as a real priority to find out about any members', not just women's, jobs? We will be taking this issue up again in the next chapter, and looking at the effect this gap between members and representatives has on women's participation. But we must still ask this question here: have male full-time officials and representatives on national committees really taken the trouble to become as well-informed about the practicalities of working *women's* lives as about the practicalities of working *men's* lives? What do you think? Use your own union experience to answer – and ask around amongst your friends too.

We still haven't looked at another aspect of the response of trade unions to the influx of women – male hostility to and suspicion of women in the trade union movement. Do you think that this hostility and suspicion really exists, or is it just what a few extremists would have you believe? We mentioned earlier the whole question of trade union desire to recruit women – as exclusion of women from the labour market has become unworkable, unions have set about recruiting women to boost membership numbers and to avoid a situation where there is a large pool of cheap non-union labour. Whatever the attitudes of trade union leaders and trade union members to the recruitment of women into the unions, pure practicalities have made this a desirable tactic for almost all unions – especially at a time when competition between unions for members is acute. So at the level of recruitment, it would be difficult to argue that suspicion and hostility would have had a marked effect in any case.

But perhaps a slightly different argument can be made about the desirability of having women *activists* in the union. Practical, tactical reasons have forced a change in trade union attitudes towards women members; is there any reason why a similar change should occur towards women as activists within the union?

Obviously if representation is bad, or even just a bit out of touch with members' wishes, the union risks a loss of membership as a result. Union representatives always come in for a certain amount of criticism from members, however good they are, but a certain way of losing support is to make a really bad mistake in judging what the membership wants.

If a succession of representatives make this sort of mistake, members may leave the union. So a union which consistently doesn't pay proper attention to keeping in touch with members' wishes will lose members – and a possible example of this might be male representatives and officials failing to keep in touch with the wishes of women members. But well-represented members don't usually leave the union, and few representatives who are even half-competent will actually make members resign by the odd mistake. If you were in a union where there already were reasonably efficient representatives with a fair amount of experience, would you bother to train new representatives to take their place? Would you do this if most of your existing representatives were men, and lots of the new members were women? Why or why not?

You may be saying that unions usually don't put a lot of effort into encouraging people to become shop-stewards, so why should we expect women to be given special help? Perhaps that underestimates how much shop-stewards and other representatives are actually encouraged to take responsibilities in the union. Ask a few shop-stewards or representatives you know whether anyone encouraged them. They may well tell you they didn't want to be the union representative, but no one else would stand, and someone else from the union eventually badgered them into it. You often find it was the union official, the factory convenor, or another shop-steward. You sometimes find that their friends or family have been active in their unions, and pushed them along. Where this may well leave women out is that once again, because women and men do different kinds of jobs, potential women activists just don't work beside experienced union representatives as a rule. Often they don't even have the same tea and dinner breaks. Why? Because most of the experienced representatives in trade unions are men at the moment. Remember that half of the women in trade unions at present have been in a union for less than ten years. How will these women break through to become representatives? If we begin to realize that we need to think hard about how to get more women to the point where they are prepared to become representatives, we are at least making a start on the problem.

Our own efforts can get to grips with this problem. One example of the impressive changes we can make was described by journalist Anna Coote in an article on women in the trade unions in the *New Statesman* in November 1980. Marisa Casares Roach is the convenor of the Transport and General Workers' Union at the Heathrow Hotel at London Airport. There are 360 union members there, half of whom are women. In the five years since she joined the union Marisa has gone from being the only woman shop-steward to being convenor of nine female and three male shop-stewards. It's no accident that more women have come forward. Marisa says:

'Of course, they don't think they can do it at first. You just have to show them they can, and stay with them. But you couldn't rely on a man to do that.'

Do you agree with her? Do you think it is always possible to get women to come forward in this way? What effect do you think these tactics would have if they were used in a union where a lot of male union members didn't like the idea of a woman representative? Or where existing male representatives didn't like working with a woman representative, or didn't trust them, or thought they couldn't possibly be really interested in the union?

Along with all this, women representatives can find all the problems with childcare and making domestic arrangements facing them as well as their members. Can you imagine a full-time official responsible for young children, or for arranging a family's meals, excusing herself from negotiations on the grounds that she has to meet the kids from school, or make everyone's tea? Or never being able to attend conferences out of town? What could unions do to make it more possible for women to become officials? Or do we just have to wait until the woman's role in the home miraculously changes?

In this chapter we have looked at the practical difficulties

118

unions face in organizing women, the way trade unions have responded to the recent growth in women's membership, and at some of the reasons why trade union structure and the practical arrangements made by trade unions might not help women to become representatives and officials. One thing we haven't looked at is why women haven't just pushed men aside and fought for trade union positions, demanding more representation for women. Why do you think this might be? We will be thinking about that question in the next chapter.

# Further reading

*Hear this brother: Women workers and union power* Anna Coote and Peter Kellner (New Statesman, 1980). This book includes statistics about women at work and in the unions, and descriptions of the changes some unions have made in the way they organize.

*Women Workers and the Trade Unions* Sarah Boston (Davis-Poynter, 1980). This is a long book, but really well worth reading. It goes back beyond the turn of the last century, and tries to work out *why* women still don't get a fair deal from the unions after a hundred years.

'Women, Work and the Trade Union Organization' Judith Hunt and Shelley Adams, (WEA, 1980) and 'Organizing Women Workers' Judith Hunt (WEA, 1975) are pamphlets produced in the WEA's *Studies for Trade Unionists* series. Both pamphlets contain a great deal of information – and are cheaper to buy than any of the other sources.

TUC Reports, especially those from the women's conferences, are very useful. Your local library should be able to get copies for you.

*In and against the State* London Edinburgh Weekend Return Group, (Pluto Press, 1980) looks at the particular problems faced by trade unionists in the public services. It gives examples of some of the ways workers have been able to fight back.

*Getting Organized* Alan Campbell and John McIlroy, and *Unions and Change Since 1945* Chris Baker and Peter Caldwell (Pan, 1981) in the same series as this book examine some of the issues raised in this chapter.

# Chapter **Five**

## Participation – our own worst enemies

We have already looked at the problems faced by women in trying to combine trade union activity with 'two jobs'. We have looked at some of the obvious organizational changes which trade unions could make to help get women involved. We have also looked at some of the ways we could use collective agreements to make participation easier for women. Is this enough? Or do you think it's a pointless exercise, and that women are their own worst enemies? Why, even when the union has gone to some trouble to make it easier for women to take part, do women *still* find it hard to fight for a larger say in union democracy, union policies, and trade union action?

Let's have a look at another side of these problems. Do

trade unions, either intentionally or through lack of thought, give women the impression that somehow the union isn't *really* meant for women? Worse, do we women think there is some sort of contradiction between being a woman and being a trade unionist? Are we afraid that if we become active in the union somehow that will make us less of a woman? These are deep questions – let's see if we can come up with some of the answers.

## 'All the lads . . .'

It's not just the practical problems we looked at in the last chapter, like times of meetings, childcare arrangements and domestic commitments, which get in the way of increased involvement in the unions by women. Nor is it just the organizational problems we looked at. There is something more subtle at work – trade unions are a man's world. Do you think that's too sweeping a statement? In your union there may be more women than men, women on most of the committees and even a few women officials. Trade unions are not exclusive men's clubs, but still operate a set of informal rules which make it more difficult for women to join in.

At a trades council meeting in Aberdeen recently, one of the items on the agenda was a report back from the delegates who had attended the STUC. One of the delegates was a woman speech therapist, and as well as giving a report on what she had done, and what she had heard as a delegate, she chose to speak out about some of the things that had made her feel angry in this particular example of the trade union 'man's world'.

'perhaps most importantly for me, as a woman trades unionist, was the fact that, in a year when the trades union movement was, on the one hand, declaring a positive interest in encouraging increased active participation by female members, and on the other, bemoaning the fact that their 'efforts' in this direction were not showing great results (there were only a handful of women delegates at the conference out of the large number of delegates there) it was obvious to me from the onset of conference that trades unionists must seriously examine the damaging sexist attitudes prevailing at conference. The declaration of women delegates' marital status on the official delegates list; the references to 'housewives' – not *all* workers – suffering through price rises; and the introduction of the only female platform speaker by referring to her marital and maternal status in the absence of any such references in regard to the male guest speakers, are but a few examples reflecting attitudes all too prevalent at Perth this year. I am sure this is a matter of concern to *all* Aberdeen trades council delegates and their branches.'

Her experiences are far from unique. As a woman you can be made to feel different – and peculiar at that – from the first words the chairman of a meeting says; 'Well, brothers – oh, and sisters too, of course . . .' or 'Can we have a bit of order please, gentlemen – not forgetting the ladies here too . . .' even if said with an air of good humour and as an attempt at a friendly welcome, can make you wish the ground would open up to swallow you – especially if everyone turns round to look for the woman in question at the mention of 'sisters' or 'ladies'! Of course, this mostly happens in meetings where women don't form a large part of the usual attendance, but even if at your own workplace and in your own branch women do form the majority, as soon as you step into the wider trade union movement you will find – as things are at the moment – that women once again shrink into a minority – a minority no one else seems quite sure how to deal with.

Every trade unionist who decides to take an active part in her or his union seems to remember the moment she or he screwed up the courage to speak for the first time in a meeting, or to offer to take on some task for the union. Can you remember your own experiences – or have you thought what it will be like? If you're a woman, and have been made to feel unusual, even by an attempt at a friendly greeting, that moment often feels even worse – most women flinch when people seem to be listening harder than usual; probably just because the sound of a woman's voice has woken some of them up after a succession of male speakers. But much worse than the experiences of those who take the plunge and start trying to take an active part is what happens to the woman or man who doesn't even get her or his point of view across to the union – eventually the member will give up and retreat into the 'apathy' activists often accuse other members of.

That's the whole point of having a representative in your workplace, of course – someone who will take up the things that concern you. Where this idea breaks down is when a member is obviously in a minority at her or his particular workplace, but is sure other members of the same union have the same problem. In this position you would have to persuade your representative to take the matter up, say at branch level, and risk getting asked to come along and say a few words yourself, or else just steel yourself to raising the matter in every way open to the individual member. That's when your determination to raise an issue meets the acid test of whether your nerve fails at the crucial moment – and if your nerve fails too often you can be well on the road to apathy.

But this whole problem isn't about individuals at all. If a union remains unaware of members' views because no positive steps are taken to encourage new or inactive members to take part, the union has none of the information it needs. Its choice of priorities will be out of line with the members' wishes, and as a result existing members will become disillusioned, and potential members will not join the union at all. The union's estimation of membership support will be wrong and settlements may be made which will infuriate members, or disputes called when support will be poor. The consequences are obvious – and disastrous.

So it's very important that the union and its representatives, from shop-stewards to the general secretary know what all the members think, not just what the most confident members think. This common problem for all trade unions takes on greater importance when you relate it to women's participation in the union.

People vary a lot in confidence. As long as the less confident members of a union have more or less the same views as the more confident members of that union, nothing will go far wrong if only the confident ones make their voices heard. Things aren't so rosy when the less confident people have different views from the more confident ones – and perhaps do different kinds of jobs, work different hours, have different responsibilities outside work and have different problems.

If the confident members, or the ones who have learnt by experience to put their point of view despite their nervousness, all happen to be men, and the less confident ones are the women, then problems will – and do – arise. The women say 'The union's got no interest in us. They don't take us seriously,' and the union says: 'The women are always complaining about what we've done wrong. But they can't seem to tell you what they want, and they never come to meetings anyway.' Once this sort of vicious circle is set up, it's hard to break out of; the next chapter gives a few ideas on the positive action which can be taken to break this circle.

What can we do as trade unionists to stop this stupid – but pretty common – situation from developing in the first place? Let's start with the thing that probably demands the least confidence and experience from the member – making sure that representatives are aware of the members' views. It's worth thinking about the things on this list to try and build up a picture of how easy it is for members to put their views across in different situations.

● How many members does each representative deal with?
● Does she or he know them all? How well?
● What happens when someone new starts work? Does the representative meet her or him?
● Does the representative do the same job as everyone she or he represents? If not, does she or he know what other people's jobs are like?
● Does the representative work on the same bonus scheme and for the same hours as the members she or he represents?
● Does the representative get paid time off to talk to members?
● Do the members get time off – or even paid time – to talk to the representative?
● Does the representative get guidance on what to do from

meetings of the members, or from conversations with individuals, or both?

● Does the representative get a chance to explain union policies to the members?

All these points are common to women and men, but have a particularly sharp impact when looked at from the point of view of women workers and male representatives.

Only a few years ago it was quite common to find groups of women workers represented by men. In the North-East Scottish fish canneries, women operating fish-cutting machines and working on a line packing fish pieces into tins would have as their representative a male labourer, fork-lift driver, or even their own chargehand! This sort of situation is on the decline now, but the obvious problems it raises, when checked against the questions above, are still around – perhaps in a more subtle form – in most workplaces.

At the next level up – in the large workplace or local branch – any problems you came across in communication between member and representative are magnified. It takes much more confidence for the member to put forward a point of view in this context, and if the representative needs special skill and sensitivity to really learn what members are thinking, the branch committee needs to be even more interested and welcoming, encouraging all members to take a full part. At this, and the higher levels of the union hierarchy, positive action to encourage participation by women members, such as special programmes of education, can begin to have a good effect. (We will be looking at this in more detail in the next chapter.)

Before we consider making special formal provisions for women members, let's see what can be done at the workplace and at the local level by taking a hard look at the way most new members learn about the union and at whether women face special difficulties. Think about what it was like when you joined your union. How much did you know about the union then? Do you know more now? How did you get to know more? Perhaps in one of these ways:

● talking to your workmates;

● going to union meetings;
● going for a drink after a meeting and getting someone to tell you what the discussion at the meeting was all about;
● reading the union newspaper, or a local newsheet;
● talking to your representative.

One way or the other, you probably ended up totally confused on several occasions before you felt you were beginning to understand. You are best not to start out with a handicap in this obstacle race whilst you find out what all the initials stand for, what the branch secretary does, what an agenda or standing orders are. If you are a woman and most of the people involved in the union are men, you do often start with a handicap.

Because of the way work is still pretty much divided up between 'men's work' and 'women's work', your workmates will probably be women, and – at the moment – likely to be less involved in the union unless someone has bothered to make good practical arrangements for meetings (as described in Chapter four) or to encourage discussion of the issues the women really care about. If this is the case, the union is not likely to be a very popular or profitable subject of conversation in the tea breaks.

If you decide to go to the meetings to find out more, you will probably find you haven't understood a lot of the business because you don't know some of the background. You can either decide to keep on going to the meetings until you *do* understand, or you can take the much more pleasant alternative of going for a drink with someone who already understands and picking their brains.

But hold on a minute – if you're a woman, in spite of the fact that you're heartily sick of being told 'well, you've got Women's Lib now', you'll probably think twice about charging off to the bar with a whole bunch of men you hardly know to try and wring information about the union out of them when you know the friendly and informative chat you're hoping for can go wrong in all sorts of ways. There's the scene where the men decide to show you who knows most about the union, and no matter how straightforward your question, end up arguing way above your head about some internal wrangle in a committee you've never heard of. Or there's the, 'It's nice to see some of you girls coming to the meetings. You just ask me which way to vote if you can't understand' response. Or the man who says, 'I hope you're not going to turn all our meetings into discussions about childcare/maternity leave/sex discrimination/abortion.' Or the woman who says, 'I find the union is very fair to women. I had no trouble getting on the branch committee,' and then swans off before telling you how, or what the branch committee does. Or, worst of all, the man who tells you in all seriousness that he would like to see more women in the union, but that they are too hysterical to be shop-stewards. (Get out of that one without becoming hysterical!) Exaggerated, yes, of course. But all those horror stories are based on things that have really happened – ask around and you'll maybe get a few more!

Probably the greatest amount of trade union education goes on in pubs and bars throughout the country – though they would probably all go bust if they changed their names to 'Trade Union Education Centre'. If women are cut out from this lively educational tradition the trade union movement must think of some better way of doing membership education for women. And women *are* excluded – discouraged by the kind of remarks we have looked at; discouraged in many parts of the country by general attitudes to women in pubs; discouraged by the response of our families if we return home late, or were seen drinking with a crowd of men. The most likely to be discouraged are those most lacking in confidence – the young women, the mothers returning to work and unsure of their place in the world. They are often the 'new starts' with whom the trade union movement could start out on the right foot – before apathy sets in and the old vicious circle of 'the women aren't interested' and 'the union doesn't care about what we think' gets going. We must think of ways in which women can learn about trade unionism – and we may also benefit by including other members who find it hard to make their voices heard, and hard to learn in the pub discussion tradition – various ethnic minorities, young workers and people who live in rural areas remote from their trade union official – and often many miles from their branch meeting and other branch members. Apathy is a problem for all trade unions – thinking about how to involve women can help to solve the problem of apathy for other members too.

## 'It's difficult to be feminine while you're shouting for your rights'

The women who said that put her finger on another important issue which might throw some light on why women don't get involved. To take part you must *want* to take part – and lots of women *don't* want to. Why? Is 'femininity' something to do with it? Do women feel that being a shop-steward is unfeminine? The magazine idea of a 'real woman' or a 'proper woman' doesn't usually include being 'interested in trade unions' along with the other ideal features – being attractive, sexy, good-tempered, a great mother, a super cook. Have you ever heard a Miss World contestant mention her trade union as an interest along with the inevitable interest in children, animals, sport, or the arts?

Obviously most women don't go around trying to be like the 'ideal women' of the magazines, or imitating Miss World. But most women do want to be *women*, not some pale sort of copy of a man. What sort of image jumps to your mind if you imagine a trade unionist? Is it different from your image of 'a nice woman'? How do you think other people would see these two characters?

Let's examine this in more detail, because if women *do* feel reluctant to get involved in the union because it's not possible to stay feminine *and* be a trade unionist, whatever we do to encourage more women into the unions will meet massive resistance. Perhaps the organizational problems of involving women members are not the whole story. If the trade unions really *are* a man's world at the moment, is it because we women *are* our own worst enemies? If so, what can be done to change this?

In Chapter one we looked at how society has a big effect

on what we women see as our skills and our talents, and on the way we train for particular jobs and expect to fit into a particular role in the family. Something just as powerful goes on while we are girls and when we become women; we learn what we should be like to be 'a proper woman'. The same thing happens to boys and men, of course – starting with 'big boys don't cry'.

For women, learning to be 'a proper woman' takes up a lot of our energy, whether we admit it or not, and whether or not we then spend a lot more time trying to *unlearn* the whole thing! It's pointless to ignore how women are portrayed by the things we see around us, or to pretend that the way we think is not affected by our surroundings. Play a few games when you're next on the bus, reading a paper, walking through town or idly watching TV and you may be surprised at what you find out. Try these:

- Look at adverts. Count how often someone who has nothing to do with the product is in the picture. Is it a woman or a man? Is the person young or old, attractive or unattractive? Is the person fully clothed?
- Count the number of times men are mentioned in newspaper articles on a particular page or pages. Do the same for women. Count the number of photographs of men and of women on the same page or pages.
- Think about who says and does what in a television film. How long do men speak for? What about women? If you really want to get sophisticated, try this one. Sometimes you see a camera shot of a face expressing some emotion or other, just for a couple of seconds before the shot swings back to the action. How often is this a woman, and how often a man? How does this compare with the total amount of time you see men and women on the screen in other kinds of shot?

If you play these games you will discover a lot of interesting facts. You'll come to the conclusion that if a Martian was supplied with a set of photos from adverts, she or he would think British Earthlings are mostly female, with a tendency to wear very few clothes, and with a most peculiar lifecycle;

129

most of us seem to be in our twenties, and to conform to a particular view of attactiveness.

You'll also discover men get into news articles more than women – not surprising, perhaps, as more people in public life are men. But can you account for there being, usually, a greater proportion of women in the photos than in the articles, even in the 'quality' papers – which claim they don't use photos of women to sell the paper?

Depending on the film you pick, you may learn quite a lot about the way the film-maker sees men and women. One funny example was a film which just happened to be on television on the very evening, some years ago, when a women's group in Aberdeen decided to take notes on a whole evening's television programmes on each channel. The film was a Western, featuring several men and one woman. She hardly appeared, except in short clips to show her expression of horror when someone was shot or the cattle stampeded. When she finally spoke – once in fifty minutes – everyone leaned forward to hear what she said. It was, 'I may be John's wife, but I'm also my fathers' daughter.' Most examples you find won't sound like such blatant propaganda, but you may be surprised that programmes you've always thought gave a lot of time to women don't work out that way when you keep an eye on your watch.

The examples you have found for yourself will perhaps have convinced you that we *do* live in a sexist society – in other words, a society in which men and women are likely to be treated differently on the basis of prejudices we have learnt and carry on learning – from when we were babies right through our lives.

Do you think things are changing now and that, although this might have been the case years ago, everyone nowadays has accepted that men and women are equal? Most of us would admit we still have some sexist prejudices, and although we may *think* men and women are equal, we still don't always *feel* that way. Which is fine when we have time to think out our point of view, but awful when we have to react quickly, or in a situation where people are getting steamed up over something.

To give you some examples, try eavesdropping on some of the things people say. Maybe you will find a bit of you that sympathizes with some of these statements, whatever you *think* about equality.

● 'Swearing sounds worse coming from a girl than a boy.'
● 'You can't have an office full of women without bitchiness.' (But you can have an office full of men without bitchiness?)
● 'Every woman really wants to settle down with a man and have a family – men just want a good time.'
● 'Boys don't like girls who are too clever.'
● 'If there's a redundancy, it's only fair for the married women to give up their jobs first.'
● 'Whatever they say, women are more interested in love, and men are more interested in sex.'
● 'I can't stand argumentative women.'

Perhaps you're trying to get a word in here that you never said there was no difference between men and women, that you just said they were equal. OK, perhaps we are different, but why? And does the way that we're different seem to point to particular problems for women? Most important of all, does believing that men and women are different make us weaker as trade unionists, by breaking our solidarity with each other or by making it more difficult for women to become active?

Let's go back and look at these questions one by one. First of all, are men and women different? (This is meant as a serious question!) Obviously we have different sorts of bodies, and obviously the fact that women can have babies is a very real and important difference affecting wide areas of many women's lives – from the plans we make to provide some sort of financial security during pregnancy and nursing, to the effort we put into making contraception work and dealing with its side-effects. But notice that the way our society works has crept into this 'simple' question. Financial security for women and children is always given as one of the reasons for marriage, and a good deal of our laws about marriage and divorce are designed to make men face up to

131

a responsibility to provide for their dependent women and children. To get back to the main point, the biological differences can't be seen in isolation from the results of a social system. It's not the fact that women have babies that makes us look to a man to provide financial security during our pregnancies and when we are looking after children. It's a system that works on the idea of a family unit with a man as the main breadwinner. (And that idea isn't even correct for all of us! One in six families has a female breadwinner.)

So we are different, but the ways in which we are different can be exaggerated by a social system which treats men and women differently or become much less important in a society where men and women were treated in the same way. Let's pursue this question a bit further by seeing why we're different in more ways than simple biology and what effect this has on the way we see ourselves as men or as women.

First of all, some men are the same as *some* women in some ways, and there are differences between women and between men. We live in a complicated world which would be hard to deal with unless we split it up into 'boxes'. We don't deal with every single person we ever come across as an individual – we put them into a mental 'box' which helps us to understand them just well enough for our particular purposes. If we know someone fits into the 'box' of 'shop assistant' we don't need to find out whether their hobbies include deep-sea diving or the study of ancient Greek before we have a rough idea of what they will do if we offer them money for something we want to buy. So these boxes can come in very handy for making sense of our world. But we make a mistake if we forget that these boxes are just handy devices for working out the usual answer. The shop assistant *might* take your money and tear it up or throw it away. She or he *might* just run off with the money. In which case, your previous ideas about shop assistants won't have been much help to you.

Sometimes it's convenient to use boxes to describe the differences between men and women. For example, we could say 'women are shorter than men' or 'men are stronger than women'. Both of these things may be true for *most* men and *most* women. But if you can't reach a high shelf would you reject an offer of help from a woman six feet tall on the grounds that men are taller than women? If you want some-one to help you move house, a strong woman will be a lot more use than a man who can't lift very much. We make mistakes of just this kind when we say 'women aren't inter-ested in the union' or 'men can stand up for themselves'.

What about particular problems that result from the way we see differences between men and women? What about this as a caricature of the way we see femininity and masculinity?

| | |
|---|---|
| passive | active |
| dependent | independent |
| emotional | rational |
| weak | strong |
| pretty | rugged |
| romantic | down-to-earth |
| helpless · | practical |
| restricted | ambitious |
| helpful | competitive |
| silly | sensible |
| sensitive | thick-skinned |
| submissive | authoritative |

Of course, it would be a joke to suggest that any of us think femininity or masculinity is as simple as that. Do you think it would be easier for someone who thought they were help-less, emotional and silly or someone who thought they were rational, strong and down to earth to put themselves forward as a trade union activist? The question isn't worth asking. It's a constant struggle as a woman activist to keep your self-confidence from being dented time after time by these faint but real prejudices. If you try and answer back, the answer is ready – 'of course I don't think women are silly' – and to an extent this is true. At a deeper level though, we have been learning a lot about what women and men are like – or supposed to be like – since childhood. You may well be a bit surprised when you see a woman garage mechanic in an oily boiler suit, or when a man tells you you will have to see his boss about something and the boss turns out to be a woman.

They just don't fit into the set of 'boxes' which limit most people's thinking. And the list of words we have looked at shows us something similar. Which of us hasn't at some time been caught out by this trick question? A boy and his father are involved in a car crash, injured and taken to the local casualty department. The duty surgeon is about to go off duty, but is called to the emergency. When the boy is brought in the surgeon says, 'Oh my God, it's my own son.' What is their relationship? (The surgeon is the boy's mother.)

Long before we know a particular woman or man as an individual, we expect them to be certain things, and do certain things, *because* they are a man or a woman. And it's not just other people we expect things from, we also use the same kind of ideas when we think about what we expect from ourselves. Before you read on, take a minute or two to take stock of what *you* think about masculinity and femininity. Are men and women expected to do different things in your union, and if so, why?

## Trade union solidarity

What has all this to do with trade union solidarity – the time-honoured principles of 'All for one, one for all' and 'Unity is strength'? Obviously the many individuals who combine together into a trade union have many different purposes in doing so. Some want better wages, some want better conditions or more holidays. Some want higher rates for more skilled or more highly trained workers. Some think that their unskilled jobs are so unpleasant that this should be reflected in a better wage than that earned by more skilled workers in more pleasant jobs.

Early on in the trade union movement it became clear that if workers did not act together they had no power. If one individual refused to work for a particularly low wage she or he could take the choice of refusing the job and earning nothing at all. But if all the workers who might have taken that job banded together and *no one* took the job until a better rate was offered, there was a chance of doing something. Even though asking everyone to turn down the chance of a wage meant worse individual hardship in the end collective action meant that the potential employer *had* to change her or his mind, or do without a work-force – not a very profitable way of running a business!

We are powerless as individual workers, but stronger the more we act together, despite the hardship or inconvenience this always creates for the individual. It has always been in employers' interests to divide us – in fact to 'divide and rule'. It can be done quite simply – by offering an individual bonus to someone who works very fast, for example; this may result in older workers not being able to earn a decent wage, as the young and strong will collect enough of a bonus not to worry that much about the basic rate. It may result in older workers trying so hard to keep up that they damage their health. It may result in safety shortcuts – and someone will in time be injured. The same thing can be done to break solidarity between unions, and this too does nothing for anyone except the employer. Offer one union at a workplace a really good deal on their annual wage claim and, if they accept, watch everyone get trampled in the rush of each union for itself.

Anyone or any group who breaks solidarity is a tremendous risk to all of us – just like a fire in a crowded cinema, if everyone thinks about others and behaves in an orderly way more people will escape to safety in the end, instead of everyone getting stuck in the scramble which results if each person tries to get her or himself out at all costs. If union members act together in everyone's interests we can change the way employers behave towards us. If some of us are bought off they, as individuals, might still benefit, but the rest of us won't. The infuriating thing is that people are often bought off for less than they would have got by sticking with everyone else – so they don't even really benefit as individuals.

These principles of unity then are crucial to the strength of the trade union movement, and to our ability to influence any situation. (This is discussed in more detail in another book in this series – *Getting Organized*.) We have looked at some well-known divisive situations – of course, setting up the men and women against each other is equally useful to the employer. The historical section of the last chapter described some trade union responses to this problem, which fell into two main types of strategy – trying to get the same conditions for women, so that there would be no need for division between male and female union members, or trying to push women back to the home, or at the very least into different kinds of work so that differences between men's and women's interests are kept conveniently out of trade union affairs.

We have to decide now which – if either – of these ways of dealing with the problem affords the best way forward for trade union members *as a whole* – men *and* women. Certainly keeping women out of trade unions has not been a noticeable success – women are not going to go back to the home; as workers, women cannot be excluded from trade unions without posing exactly the same threat to trade union organization as any large non-union group would pose. Making a genuine attempt to take account of the interests of women members is both less divisive from an organizational point of view and more likely to result in better conditions for everyone.

This comes back again to differences between men's interests and women's interests. Trade unions have pursued men's interests for well over a century – and have come to regard men's interests as trade union interests. Instead of doing what the early trade unionists had to do, and in each situation working out what was best for a particular group of workers, we now have the advantage of being able to look back and see what trade unions have done in the past. This is great – it saves us always having to start from scratch. But it also limits the way we think about what trade unions are *for*. The membership of trade unions is changing. There are a lot more women involved now, but very little history of fighting for conditions which are the genuine trade union issues for women – not 'women's issues' any more than a fight to improve sick pay is an 'unhealthy person's issue'. Anything which affects any worker's conditions affects all of us – dividing up problems into issues which relate to individuals or to special groups is just an example of 'divide and rule'.

We are much easier victims of the 'divide and rule' strategy if we let our own prejudices about men and women undermine our knowledge as trade unionists that unity is all-important. Not unity in the sense of us all being the same, or all having the same interests, but unity in the sense of being prepared to act together to protect our own and each other's interests. The idea that women are frivolous makes it harder for us to persuade other trade unionists to support us unless everyone is prepared to challenge their prejudices, and look at who benefits from us hanging on to sexist prejudices.

Sexist prejudices won't just go away if we ignore them. We will have to actively encourage women members to participate and we must discuss with new activists the conflicts they will feel between what they have been told is the right way for a woman to behave and the way they will need to behave to get things done through the union. We need to spend time explaining that certain issues are not 'just' women's issues; but are trade union issues, even though on occasion everyone affected by a particular issue may be a woman. We need to emphasize that support given to women trade unionists is *not* a generous gift from a well-organized group to a badly organized group, but an essential part of trade union solidarity. We need to point out the irrationality in referring to maternity rights as a 'women's issue' and low pay as a 'trade union issue' when both issues most directly affect women, and indirectly affect everyone. We must fight 'women's issues' being shunted off to special committees so that the rest of the union doesn't have to 'waste time' on them. We must look at the way our ideas about femininity prevent us passing on information to new women activists and think about ways to improve education and training for women activists. Most important of all we must recognize that sexism, however innocent and trivial it may seem in one situation, is actually powerful enough to break trade union solidarity if we leave it unchallenged.

*Sexism – the spanner in the works*

The ideas we have just been discussing may help us to understand why some of the best-intentioned efforts of trade unions to involve women have gone wrong. If deep-seated prejudices go unchallenged, there is no point in trying to make changes on the surface. If whenever a woman becomes active in the union we refer to her as 'a woman trade unionist' rather than 'a trade unionist', have we accepted her as a real trade unionist? Would we refer to a man as 'a man trade unionist'? Why don't we? If we refer to some issues as 'trade union issues' and to others as 'women's issues', which do you think will get the most attention at a meeting where there is much to discuss, and something is going to have to be shelved? How would you feel if you were the woman trying to raise the 'women's issue', and other people were urging you to let the meeting get on with the 'main' business?

Let's bear this in mind, and have a look at two things that are common in the unions – the 'token woman', and the women's committee. Would women become 'tokens' if it wasn't for sexism? Would women's committees be different if it wasn't for sexism?

**The token woman** Have you heard: 'It would be nice to have a woman on this committee' or 'We have a woman on our National Executive' or 'We've always had a woman on our delegation'? What does this mean? Do you agree with this woman trade unionist? She has been a feminist for a long time.

I used to think, when I first became interested in the trade union movement in the early 1970s, that it was a really good sign that most unions seemed to have a few women on their committees. I thought that meant a breakthrough for women was on its way, and that in a few years there would be lots more women around the committees and delgations of the trade unions. As I learnt more, I was surprised to find that many of the women I had assumed were the first few of a movement had in fact often been on the committees for years already. Worse, there didn't seem to be that many more women coming forward. I began to worry that as soon as there was

someone to 'put the women's point of view', that was it – there was
no need to involve more women.

Having a token women perhaps meant that everyone could
say, 'Jean deals with all that' about any 'women's issue'. It
perhaps meant any accusations that the union did not take
women seriously could be dealt with by saying 'but Jean's
our branch secretary/delegate to congress/expert on new
technology'. It perhaps meant that whenever a request for a
speaker on equal pay, or maternity rights, or women's rights,
or abortion came to a trade union, someone said, 'Jean can
do that'. What it also probably meant was that every time
Jean stood up to speak, someone, somewhere said 'There
goes Jean, on about women again.' Does everyone heave a
sigh of relief when one woman gets involved? At last there
will be no more uncomfortable silences when someone asks
what the union does for women, or how many women are
involved. What often happens is that the 'token woman' gets
landed with having to be an expert on all issues which affect
women *and* having to be a really good trade unionist – she
is always on show as an example of a woman involved in
the union, and often feels she has to be twice as good as a
man for just this reason.

Token women tend to be very conscious of 'going on about
women again' and of being asked to be the woman on various
committees and delegations, whether they happen to know
anything about the subject or not. What would you have
done in these situations?

It was getting very late, and we were still discussing the motions
we wanted to send to conference. We had one motion in about the
Employment Act, and I suddenly noticed we were suggesting the
whole thing should be thrown out. Well, in general I agreed, but
the Employment Act has given one new right to women which I
happen to think is very important – the right to time off to go to
ante-natal clinic if you're pregnant. Lots of kids are born unhealthy
who could have been born healthy with the right ante-natal care,
not to mention the mother's well-being. So I suggested an amend-
ment. It was really difficult to get the wording to make sense, and
several people suggested that we ought to have a motion that was
easy to understand, and that we should perhaps leave out my

suggestion so that we could get on. I was on the point of agreeing when I happened to catch another woman's eye, and thought 'Why should I give up? No one else would give up if it was their particular trade that was getting a good deal out of one section of the Act.' We eventually managed to get it included, but I felt everyone must be fed up with me.

We were sending a delegation to talk to the Housing Department. Someone suggested that a woman should be on the delegation. None of the women at the meeting knew anything about housing, and there were lots of the men who did. It would have been daft for one of us to volunteer, but I bet they were all thinking we just weren't interested. Obviously, housing does affect women a lot, and I do wonder about how much our delegates had thought about the issue from a woman's point of view. That's what is important, not just trailing a woman along.

What can you achieve as a token woman in the trade union movement? You tend to make only superficial changes unless there is real interest and involvement from other women in the union to give you support. In the early part of this century, as part of the wider struggle for women's rights, lots of women tried to – and did – influence the direction of the trade union movement. (There's more on this in the chapter on 'Women fighting back'.) These women have left their mark, but the changes they might have made didn't go as far as they might have hoped. Was this because they fell into the 'token woman' trap? If so, what must we do to follow on from the new struggle for women's rights in the late sixties and seventies to make sure it doesn't happen again?

**'Perhaps the women's committee could make the teas . . .'**
Another way forward for women in trade unions has an unfortunate habit of turning into a blind alley. Women's committees have done a great deal of good work in the unions, but considering that some of them have been on the go for years, the impact they have made on trade union thinking or on the public image of the trade union movement seems quite small. Why is this? Is sexism at work again?

We have already looked at some of the problems of confidence which face new activists in the trade unions – and women in particular. One idea to cope with this is to let women find a place and develop confidence in an all-female group. This seems like a good idea. Some of the problems about getting hold of the kind of information people tell you in the pub can be got round. Fears of appearing unfeminine when standing up for something you believe in are perhaps less important and the feeling of being on show just because you're a woman goes away. You can try your wings at a women's conference, perhaps trying out making a speech and using a microphone. Certainly the women's committees have produced good women activists who have moved on to the wider trade union movement, but not many. Why not?

Firstly, the women's committee and women's conferences can become a substitute for involvement in the union as a whole, taking up all your time and energy. Secondly, you may only get to develop your ideas on 'women's issues' – the 'real' issues still get discussed only in the union as a whole. Everyone wants to know what the women's committee thinks about maternity rights – there's not the same interest in the women's committee's views on the annual wage negotiations.

Secondly, the women's committee gets asked to make the teas! Seriously, it does still happen. Here's an example.

I was talking on women's rights to a local Labour Party branch. I thought I must have said something awful when all the women walked out – but, no, they had gone to make the tea. The worst thing was that the talk was supposed to give the women members a chance to discuss something that affected them directly – but no one had thought to change the structure of the meeting.

'Making the teas' is just an illustration of what happens when it is forgotten that the reason women are at a meeting is as people interested in that meeting *not* as women who have happened to come along. The idea of women's domestic role is so strong that even when women are somewhere for a reason that has nothing to do with housework we are still assumed to be 'on duty' as housewives, and available for all kinds of housework – making teas, cleaning up, running the crèche, arranging jumble sales, and so on. Of course, everyone has some special skill or talent which the union will want to use, and no one would suggest that these jobs – the 'housework' – do not need to be done. But why not rotate the jobs? Why make someone miss part of the meeting so that the teas arrive with no delay, rather than waiting a bit longer at the break?

Once again, sexist prejudices can dramatically alter what appears to be a good idea. Women's committees can be wrecked on the rocks of 'women's issues' or of enforced domesticity. Some have escaped – many individual women activists have benefited from the women's committee structure. Special groups for women are not a magic wand.

**Overcoming diffidence – positive training** We have to recognize the importance of sexism and positively organize to fight it. Sexist ideas are all around us and influence our trade union activities unless we constantly think hard. Part of the struggle is convincing men in the trade union movement that it's not a case of there being 'women's issues' – which don't really concern them, and 'trade union issues' – which do. But a bigger part is women fighting our battles, demanding to be taken seriously as trade unionists and regarding our interests as legitimate trade union interests, not 'side issues'. To play this part we need more confidence, and more skill.

How can we get more confidence and skill, and use it most effectively? Is the answer to provide education and practical experience for women? The next chapter goes on to describe some of the ways this can be done.

# Further reading

*What Society Does to Girls* Joyce Nicholson (Virago, 1977). This book outlines the way that girls and women learn to be feminine. It's a simply written, clear introduction, and doesn't use jargon from psychology or sociology.

*The Gender Trap Book 3: Message and images* Carol Adams and Rae Laurikie-tus (Virago, 1980 (revised)). This part of *The Gender Trap* takes a hard look at what advertisers, schools, jokes, films and our friends and families would have us believe it's like to be a woman. The glamorous sex-symbol, the deodourized person, the super-mum, the sympathetic ear . . . and perhaps all at once!

*Connexions: His and Hers* Joy Groombridge (Penguin, 1971) is a useful book designed for schools and colleges, discussing masculinity and femininity and the ways we see them. It's a bit out of date now, but the ideas are still good.

*Getting Organized* Alan Campbell and John McIroy (Pan, 1981) talks about some of the issues we have looked at in a broader way.

*'Just like a girl': How girls learn to be women* Sue Sharp (Penguin, 1976). This is an interesting book, based on a survey of London schoolgirls, which looks at the whole set of pressures shaping these girl's lives. Education and work prospects get an especially close look.

# Chapter **Six**

## Women fighting back

We have looked now in this book at the jobs women do, at the rough deal women get from education and training for work, at domestic responsibilities, at the pay and conditions and opportunities open to women at work, and at problems in trade union organization and attitudes. What needs to be done? Can we act to change the position of women in the trade union movement? How likely are we to succeed? What will happen to the trade unions if we can't make these changes? These are big questions, and ones that will need a lot of discussion by trade unionists. Let's at least have a look at these questions in this last chapter.

## Positive action

One of the great fears expressed by women who opposed the Conservative proposals for a Sex Discrimination Act in the early seventies was that there was no provision for 'positive discrimination', and that the Act would therefore make it difficult for anyone who wanted to improve things for women. The version of the Act that finally became law *did* allow some positive discrimination, and many unions have now begun to use this part of the Act.

So what *is* 'positive discrimination'? The whole idea is pretty difficult to describe in the abstract, but quite easy to understand if we look at a few examples.

Let's take up one of the things we have already looked at – the small number of girls who take up apprenticeships. If we look at opportunities to take up engineering, girls and boys should now have the same chance of getting an apprenticeship, as the Sex Discrimination Act forbids employers to discriminate. How long is it going to take before girls begin to get these apprenticeships in large numbers? There's nothing standing in their way – or is there?

● Girls choice of school subjects may be along traditional lines – maybe leaving them short of qualifications in sciences, maths and technical subjects.
● Careers teachers and advisors haven't been transformed overnight by the Sex Discrimination Act. They are probably still more likely to think of suggesting engineering to a boy than to a girl.
● Job Centres are the same. Although they may try not to discriminate, there are still plenty of examples where advisors say, 'I'll tell you about this job, but I don't think it would really suit you', to a girl or woman.
● Family and friends may well have a different reaction to a boy's *sensible* choice of an engineering apprenticeship and a girl's *unusual* choice of the same thing.
● Boys will probably know a grown man who has done an apprenticeship of the kind they want. Girls are much less likely to know a woman who can tell them what their

apprenticeship was like – unless, of course, it was in hairdressing!

Maybe girls *do* face a few extra difficulties and probably this will slow down progress towards equality – especially in times of rising unemployment, when to talk of a choice of jobs at all is a cruel joke for many young people, with loads of people chasing too few jobs. Employers will require higher qualifications and recruit well-known types of candidates for jobs rather than trying out something new – taking on girls, perhaps.

To help girls along in this kind of situation what would you do?

- Encourage schools, careers advisors and so on to give girls a wider choice of school subjects and possible jobs.
- Provide special training for girl school leavers to bring them up to the standards required by employers.
- Give preference to girls when choosing people for training courses.
- Give preference to girls for jobs.

The last three of these things would be illegal if we had a Sex Discrimination Act which said girls and boys (or women and men) must always be treated exactly the same. Our Sex Discrimination Act does *not* allow positive action to select girls or women for jobs, but *does* allow girls to be given preference in terms of training.

You may have spotted that all the suggestions we just looked at *cost money* – training is expensive, and so is promoting any scheme in schools, or retraining advisors. Some lucky girls have had special training, for example on courses sponsored by the Engineering Employers Federation. But not much has been done in this line – perhaps it's not really surprising when we look at how employers are trying to cut costs nowadays. Special job training for girls is one example of the possible uses of positive discrimination – treating whichever sex is getting the worst deal better to encourage faster progress towards equality.

Our example came from the area of training for jobs, but

146

it's also legal to take some forms of positive action within the unions. Positive action could be taken to improve the position of *men* in a union if they were under-represented as officials, or on decision-making bodies, but in practice it's usually women who are under-represented, so let's stick to talking about women – though all the comments about the law of course apply to men in a similar situation.

## Positive action in the unions.

The Sex Discrimination Act allows trade unions to take these kinds of positive action quite legally:

● Special action to encourage women to become members, if comparatively few women have been members in the last twelve months.
● Special training for women if few women have held particular posts in the union.
● Special encouragement – for example, campaigns – to encourage women to take up posts within the union that few women hold.
● Special steps to make sure that elected union executives, committees or conferences include a reasonable number of women, for example by reserving a certain number of seats for women.

But it is still *not* lawful to:

● Discriminate between men and women when *appointing* someone to a union post, for example as shop-steward.
● Reserve a certain proportion of posts as, for example, shop-steward for women.
● Allow only women the right to vote for certain members of committees or other elected bodies.

As you have no doubt seen for yourself, it's a pretty fine line between what's legal and what isn't. Let's just recap:

● Women *can* get special training and be given special encouragement to apply for union posts.
● You *can't* take a woman rather than a man just because

147

she's a woman when you are actually selecting someone for a post – you must treat the men who have applied in the same way as you treat the women who have applied.

● *For elected bodies only* you can reserve a certain number of seats for women, but you must allow all members to vote for all possible candidates, in other words, you can't just let the men vote for male candidates, and the women for female candidates.

What do you think of all this? Some people say the whole idea is just a waste of time. Others say women have always had an equal chance to come forward, so why all the fuss? Other people again say the law doesn't go nearly far enough, and that to give women experience in the union you should be able to give them union posts in preference to men whenever they apply.

Where do *you* stand on this issue? What is your union's policy on positive discrimination? Does your union take any of the special kinds of action we have looked at? Do you think this kind of action is having the desired effect in your union? Would you like to see more or less of this kind of action? Or does no one know what your union's policy is, or whether any special action is being taken? (If you want to find out, ask your representative or branch secretary to look into the question for you if they can).

When you have made up your own mind what you think about this, have a look at the TUC Charter on Equality for Women within Trade Unions which is reprinted opposite. How far does the Charter go? What do you think of the Charter? If unions take it seriously, will it help women in the unions? Will the unions take it seriously?

You will see the Charter covers quite a few different things. It mentions *practical arrangements* for meetings, such as paid time off, and childcare facilities where they are needed. It suggests that the *public image* of the union should include a commitment to involving women in union activities at all levels, and that all union publications should take care to avoid sexism. Special emphasis on training for women is recommended. And, most importantly, union democracy is

# A TUC CHARTER

**1** The National Executive Committee of the union should publicly declare to all its members the committment of the union to involving women members in the activities of the union at all levels.

**2** The structure of the union should be examined to see whether it prevents women from reaching the decision-making bodies.

**3** Where there are large women's memberships but no women on the decision-making bodies special provision should be made to ensure that women's views are represented, either through the creation of additional seats or by co-option.

**4** The National Executive Committee of each union should consider the desirability of setting up advisory committees within its constitutional machinery to ensure that the special interests of its women members are protected.

**5** Similar committees at regional, divisional, and district level could also assist by encouraging the active involvement of women in the general activities of the union.

**6** Efforts should be made to include in collective agreements provision for time off without loss of pay to attend branch meetings during working hours where that is practicable.

**7** Where it is not practicable to hold meetings during working hours every effort should be made to provide child-care facilities for use by either parent.

**8** Child-care facilities, for use by either parent, should be provided at all district, divisional and regional meetings and particularly at the union's annual conference, and for training courses organized by the union.

**9** Although it may be open to any members of either sex to go to union training courses, special encouragement should be given to women to attend.

**10** The content of journals and other union publications should be presented in non-sexist terms.

emphasized – unions are asked to check that women can in practice reach the decision-making bodies, to find ways of making sure women's views are represented on decision-making bodies, either by reserving seats, or by asking extra women to join committees (co-option). Further involvement of women through special advisory committees at various levels should also be considered, says the Charter.

**Special advisory committees** It may strike you as a bit strange that the Charter calls for special advisory committes to look at the particular concerns of women members, at the same time as unions are fighting for equality between the sexes at work. We looked at how women fare in the usual trade union structure in Chapter four, and you will remember how women are under-represented among the officials and committees of unions. Special advisory committees might give women a voice – but the whole issue is a bit of a hot potato in the unions at the moment. In Chapter five we looked at the ways women's committees can go astray. The TUC Women's Advisory Committee has been going for fifty years – perhaps we can get some useful ideas about positive action by looking at its history.

The Women's Advisory Committee of the TUC has seen many changes of opinion since it was established in 1930 after a special women's conference. Recruitment of members generally had been a major problem for the unions in the late twenties, and women's recruitment problems had been submerged for a few years during attempts to boost membership generally. At the same conference it was recommended that there should be local organizing committees, as sub committees of trades councils, with special responsibility for recruiting new women members and keeping the interest of women who were already trade unionists. Unions were also encouraged to form branch committees to discuss the recruitment of women. (Is any of this beginning to sound familiar?)

What effects did those proposals have? By 1932, the Women's Advisory Committee reported that, having circulated 421 trades councils with the proposals, most of them (286) had not even replied, sixty-five of the rest reported that no action had been taken, thirty-five were considering the proposals, and thirty-five were able to say that they *had* formed a committee. Apart from apathy of local officials of trade unions the Women's Advisory Committee also blamed fear of victimization during the intense industrial depression for the lack of action. Perhaps the Women's Advisory Committee could have been partly to blame too – they had not given much practical advice on how to go about recruitment of women or how to interest women in the unions in their letters. In particular they had not identified positive aims for women workers which would bring women into the unions with a real purpose.

Unfortunately when positive aims for women workers *were* sorted out later in the 1930s, these aims turned out to be 'Health and Beauty' – to be achieved by *better wages* for nourishing food and nice clothes, *shorter hours*, with more time for rest, exercise and getting fresh air, and *better conditions*, including safety, at work. Of course, there's nothing at all wrong with better wages, shorter hours or good working conditions! But were women workers *really* more likely to be interested in these gains if they thought they were a route to 'Health and Beauty', or does the whole campaign reveal the sexist attitudes of both male and female trade unionists – that all women workers fitted into a well-known stereotype – the woman who wouldn't really be interested in anything as important as trade unionism, or as practical as better wages and conditions, but could be relied on to take her appearance seriously?

There was one serious flaw in these efforts – a failure to recognize a real contradiction. Along with trying to recruit women through expensive publicity campaigns, many unions continued to offer women a bad deal when they *did* join – everything from fighting to keep demarcation between 'men's work' and 'women's work', to agreeing wage rates that were good for men and bad for women, to refusing to believe that women really wanted to join the union at all. When unions did take up the concerns of women members they were rewarded by genuine interest from the women in union affairs. When they failed to recruit and take notice of

151

women, many unions ended up with their organization dreadfully weakened by the availability of cheap female non-union labour to their employers.

Just as in the late seventies, the efforts of the Women's Advisory Committee in the 1930s were set against a background of recession, difficulties for industry, and increasing automation – though in the 1930s the main focus of trade union concern was men's jobs being automated to the point where women and young people could take them over. In the eighties the major threat of new technology may well be to women's jobs.

What lessons can we learn from our brief look at history? (If you would like to know more of the detail read Sarah Boston's book, *Women Workers and the Trade Unions*. The chapter entitled 'Asking for Bread and Getting a Stone' deals with the years from 1923 to 1939.)

## Positive action in the 1930s – what went wrong?

The positive action of the 1930s didn't work out as well as the Women's Advisory Committee had hoped. Women didn't join the unions in huge numbers, and men stayed in the spotlight of trade union action with women and their concerns well into the sidelights. Here's a list of some ideas which could explain the lack of success – can you think of other reasons? Was it that women didn't want to respond to the Advisory Committee's efforts?

● The Women's Advisory Committee were out of touch with what most trade unionists wanted and tried to foist their ideas about women's equality on to the trade unions.
● Women workers genuinely didn't want to join trade unions.
● Women were unwilling to take action, either against employers, or to improve their position within the union.
● Women didn't know how to go about getting involved with the union.

Or was it that trade unions still weren't prepared to make women a priority?

- Trade union officials and trade union members didn't think it was important to attract women members.
- Trade union officials thought they would lose the support of existing members if they spent more time on women members.
- Economic recession and the fear of losing jobs made trade unions 'play safe' and regard protecting men's jobs as more important than improving conditions for women at that time.
- Unions were unwilling to change their ideas of what kind of issues were their concern. The different issues raised by women members were not regarded as *real* trade union issues.

Or was it that the trade unions didn't really seem able to help women?

- Women were interested in improving their conditions at work, but didn't think the trade unions could help.
- Women tried to improve their conditions though trade unions, but became frustrated by the lack of success.
- Once in the union, women never seemed to get into positions where they could influence decisions.

Or had no one thought about domestic responsibilities?

- Unions did not make practical arrangements which might have helped women with domestic responsibilities to fit in trade union activities around at least two jobs.
- Women didn't want improved conditions at work because they still thought their *real* role was in the home.

Which of these reasons do you think are the most likely to be to blame for the failure to involve more women workers in the unions? And – the million dollar question – are any of the same issues going to get in the way of women's involvement in trade unions now? What does this experience tell us about positive action? Is positive action useful?

One thing that *is* significant is that in the 1930s women workers *did* tend to join the 'unofficial' trade unions – the 'red' unions refused affiliation to the TUC and mostly supported by the Communist Party and the National Minority

Movement, who aimed to challenge the traditional craft union tactics of restrictive practices and preserving sectionalism. These tactics had never been open to women workers, who lacked the skilled status necessary to use them. The Minority Movement unions didn't do that much about women's equality either, but their different style of organization was often more appealing to women workers than the official TUC-affiliated unions – much to the concern of the TUC. So perhaps organizational style *is* crucial – and women did join and become active in unions which they felt could help them.

Perhaps the failure of positive action in the 1930s has given efforts to involve women a bad name. Women's interests got shunted off to the women's advisory committees while the men got on with the real business, possibly accompanied by a couple of women. Disillusion with the lack of progress from women's conferences and women's advisory committees led to the kind of thinking which Yvonne Richards put into words at the TUC annual conference in 1971:

We are a divided body because we have a divided TUC for women. I am a woman and I have listened to discussion on a great many topics that do not directly concern me, but I know that they concern me in an overall fashion . . . I also know that my brothers are equally capable of taking an interest in topics that concern women in this organization. The only people who can benefit from any division, whether it is a well-intentioned or a rather mindless one, are the employers. We say we are united, we say unity is strength, let us show it be throwing out the women's TUC.

Do you agree with her – or think she is in danger of throwing out the baby with the bathwater? Let's look at her argument. She has a strong line on unity, and is quite right that disunity only benefits employers. But will the problem be solved by disbanding the women's TUC and trusting that the brothers who are 'equally capable of taking an interest in topics that concern women' will in fact do so? Men have a pretty gloomy record on fighting for women's rights as a priority over more immediate trade union demands if it comes to the push. But there's a quick answer for that too – women's advisory committees haven't been able to stop that happening either.

154

*Women's* Conferences can pass resolutions, *Women's* Advisory
Committees can report and advise, but in the end it's not
these decisions which make *union* policy, but decisions made
at *union* conferences or by the *union* executive.

Is the answer to abandon special union structures for
women and force issues which might have been raised
through the women's organization within the union through
the ordinary union policy-making channels instead? Or are
the people right who say this means the issues will never be
raised at all? The decision which has to be made is whether
special channels for issues concerning women are worth having at all, perhaps in a changed form, or whether, like
Yvonne Richards in 1971, we should decide to get rid of them
if we can. Let's bring back in the TUC Charter on Equality
for Women within Trade Unions again, and have a look at
some of the ideas that have been tried out by some unions
and at how well they have worked.

## Internal union democracy

The TUC Charter recommends a public declaration of commitment to involving women from each union – there doesn't
seem to be any objection to this simple idea, and many of
the unions like NUPE and AUEW (TASS) which have managed to recruit many new women members have even used
advertisements in women's magazines to get this message
across – thankfully not using the old 'health and beauty'
slogans, but stating real aims for women workers. But, however fine such public declarations, no woman will take them
very seriously if she goes on to get involved in the union and
discovers that the union publications – from leaflets to newspapers – are full of jokes about women, references to 'member's wives' and so on. Unfortunately some unions still *do*
publish this kind of stuff, even if they don't go to the lengths
of the National Union of Miners and use pin-ups to sup-
posedly encourage members to read the union paper.

After taking these few simple steps to prevent all but the
most determined women from giving up and going home as
soon as they have anything to do with the union, it's possible

to look at how women can become more involved by doing other things suggested by the Charter – perhaps firstly by looking at union structure and whether the structure itself prevents women from reaching decision-making bodies. You may be saying 'whatever has union structure to do with it? Every member can stand for election to union posts'.

Is this true in practice? It may be, but it could also be that, for example, branch officials usually come from a few big concerns with heaps of members – not for any particular reason, except that they know more of the members, and may be more in touch with what's going on in the union if they have good workplace organization. This might mean that less women get elected if they come from smaller workplaces, as is often the case. District, divisional or regional representatives from branches may have to be prepared to travel miles to get to meetings in some distant town. Even if crèche facilities are provided, carting children about cross-country on public transport is no fun. Even for women without children, with good childcare arrangements, or with grown-up children it may be difficult to fit in attendance at this kind of meeting with domestic chores. This may mean women find it more difficult to join in at this level – making it impossible to gain the necessary experience to go on to higher-level decision-making bodies. Obviously, no one is deliberately keeping women out – but some women *are* kept out in practice.

What positive action could be taken here? Obviously some changes in practical arrangements would help – and perhaps a bit of extra encouragement for women wouldn't go amiss to help women overcome some of the extra hassle.

If this sort of action doesn't miraculously result in lots of women standing for decision-making committees within the union, the Charter recommends that committees which find themselves without women members should co-opt extra women, or create extra seats reseved for women, as is already done in various unions – for example COHSE (The Confederation of Health Service Employees), NUPE (the National Union of Public Employees) and the TGWU (Transport and General Workers' Union.) Some unions have had reserved seats for years – and still managed to shove women's issues to one side. Why?

- A lone woman on a committee will find it pretty hard going to effectively put the 'women's point of view' on everything. (We looked at this in Chapter five.) No one can be expert in every area – or talk on every item of business. Too often there have been only one or two 'women's seats', inevitably leading to this problem, however good the particular women representatives are.
- If the women in reserved seats have no organized links to women union members they may get out of touch with the issues that concern the ordinary women union member.
- Women in this position can be outvoted! However politely women members' views are listened to, other priorities may win the day – as the long history of equal pay shows.

The Charter also recommends consideration of national, regional, divisional, and district advisory committees on the special interests of women members. Lots of women activists can tell you bitter tales of good discussions at these committees, helpful policy recommendations and real concern for women members. The bitterness comes in when they tell you what happened to their decisions – ignored or changed by the committees who actually make policy. Other women will tell you how, for example, discussion of childcare in these committees and reports made by them *have* actually changed union policy. Obviously a women's advisory committee or Equal Opportunities committee is not a magic wand. Some work, very well, some don't. But they are more likely to work if:

- They work in close cooperation with the appropriate level of formal union organization (e.g. with the district committee for district advisory committees or National Executive for the National Advisory Committee.)
- Some of the people on the advisory committee are also members of the appropriate policy-making body. This helps communication a lot, helps to prevent issues raised

157

by women getting 'lost', and often promotes real discussion and understanding.

One further barrier to women's participation may be a real lack of knowledge, experience or skills. The Charter advocates encouragement of women to attend union training courses, but doesn't tackle the difficult question of whether there should be separate courses for women. Some unions run special courses for women, and the Scottish TUC has done so too. Until 1980, the TUC had shied away from running special courses for women on a day release basis (paid time off from work), although weekend and evening courses had been run under the TUC scheme.

## Positive action through trade union education

Do women have special training needs? In the last chapter we looked at pubs as centres for trade union education at its most informal – and possibly at its best! We all learn most from people we can get to tell us about how they would deal with some problem which is really bothering us – even if we decide their ideas are rubbish in the end it's the discussion that helps. How can women get this kind of information on, and chance to discuss, trade union affairs?

Let's look at what courses are available for trade unionists at the moment, and see how useful they are to women who already are active in the union, or who might become active. The biggest single source of trade union education is the TUC scheme, which offers representatives courses which qualify for paid release from work. The courses range from introductory ones to health and safety and courses on more specialized topics – bargaining information, rights at work, new technology, and so on. Women have not come forward in great numbers for these courses, although, obviously, many women have been through TUC courses. By asking women why this might be, you can come up with quite a range of different reasons:

● 'I was afraid I would be the only woman on the course.'
● 'I work part time so I can get home to meet the kids from

158

school. I just can't spend a whole day at a course when I usually get home soon after three o'clock. There aren't any part-time courses in my area, and besides the courses are held right across the other side of town, which isn't much use from the point of view of taking care of the kids either.'

● 'Some of the other women have been on courses, but they didn't seem to get much out of them – most of the other people came from big factories where the union was really strong. They didn't seem to have the same problems as we do at all – in fact they didn't seem to think the sort of things we worry about are really things for the trade union at all. And as well, they just said, "you surely don't let management get away with that! You must have an awful union." They didn't seem to realize the problems we have just getting members to speak up for themselves.'

● 'There are lots of women at my work who would really come on a lot if they got to go on a course. But management won't give anyone except the reps day release, and most of these women won't become reps because they say they don't know enough. It's a vicious circle.'

● 'Management here have always been pretty good about release for courses. We've had mostly men shop-stewards in the past, and lots of them want to go on advanced courses as well as the introductory course. Management *do* put their foot down about how many people are off on courses at the same time. At the stewards' meetings, the lads are all shouting to get off on another course, and the women tend to give in, and put off going on a course at all – some of them find it hard with the kids to look after, others are a bit scared they will find the course too hard anyway, and some of their husbands don't take too kindly to them getting involved in the union – specially if it means getting their own tea as she's late home from the course.'

There are lots of practical points here – times and places for courses, organization to make sure of day release and course content to make sure that the courses do serve the special needs of women members. (The TUC day release courses were tried out first on well-organized, mostly male shop-stewards – and it shows!) Alongside these practical problems run problems of confidence – fear of being the only woman on the course, of being ignorant about 'real' trade unionism, or just of finding the course too difficult. How can these problems be solved?

The practical problems are probably easiest and, apart from day release, can be solved by just setting up courses a bit differently and improving the materials used by tutors on courses – and getting the tutors to take women seriously! Day release *is* a bit of a vicious circle – without good organization you can't get paid time off work for training, and without training it's that much harder to build good organization. At the moment the law does help to get representatives release, but this is no good for potential representatives. Unions have to begin to think of this as a priority for agreements if more women are to be involved.

The problems of confidence are that much harder. Throughout this book we have talked about the way women's confidence is undermined by the schools, our families, employers, the media – in fact by the way our whole system works! To expect women to just shake this all off and rush off to take union responsibility is perhaps a bit unrealistic. Courses must take practical steps to improve confidence – how can this be done?

● learning new skills;
● discussing ideas;
● becoming better informed;
● seeing that women *can* be good trade unionists;
● discovering that other women and perhaps men too are not that confident either and deciding to try to help and support each other.

In practical terms on the skills side, this probably means learning to speak up in a group, to listen to what someone is saying and be able to note down the main points, to plan out how to make a speech or explain something complicated, and to have an idea of how to tackle particular problems.

Fear of ignorance has to be tackled on two fronts – by actually learning how to get information and use it, and by showing that everyone has some subjects they know about and some they don't. Women sometimes find this easier in a women-only course than in a mixed classes. Women are sometimes afraid of showing themselves up in front of men, and find that other women can be quite supportive as they try their wings. One student who attended a women-only course said:

The course would encourage me to take up union activities further, because where I thought people might find my views and opinions boring, I've found by speaking over the table I've had quite a favourable reaction.

The extent to which women trade unionists often *do* lack confidence is shown by the comment of another woman on the same course:

I don't know if I will take up union work, but I will be able to put over my point of view to representatives, which I don't think I could have done in the past.

There's a lot of discussion at the moment about the best sort of courses for women trade unionists – does your union have a point of view? Should courses for women prepare students for attending ordinary day-release courses, or should separate courses be arranged? Is there a need for a different kind of advanced course relating to women and trade union organization, women's rights, or the special interests of women trade union members? Should all courses, for men and women, take more notice of the different concerns of women and of the different organizational problems which relate to the nature of women's work and to domestic responsibilities?

Education and training can be a powerful tool to improve union organization. To be of real use to women in the unions, education must tackle fear of appearing ignorant, fear that issues which concern members are just 'women's issues' not *real* trade union issues at all, and fear that women *can't* be good representatives and can't win the trust of men in particular, and also provide a real opportunity to learn how to speak up and argue a case competently. Education at its best

161

is an antidote to apathy – apathy is often caused by a sense of not being able to do anything about the situation anyway.

## What use is positive action?

In this chapter we have looked at various kinds of positive action – on recruitment, involvement in union activities, involvement in decision-making, and training and education. We have looked at how some ideas have been tried in the past and at the ways they have – or haven't – worked. The most important question has also been raised – will the unions take the whole question of positive action seriously? Has the Charter on Equality for Women within Trade Unions been agreed because it doesn't take any effort to pass a resolution at a conference, because everyone reckons nothing will happen anyway, or because the penny has really dropped at last that women's involvement is crucial to the survival of the trade unions?

Equality – like any other trade union issue – can be ignored if no one is actively pushing for it. What chance do you think we have of strengthening the trade union movement by the real involvement of women and of bringing about some change in the position of women?

# Fighting for our rights – the story so far

Women have been prepared to cause a lot of trouble this century in fighting for our rights – and we sometimes forget what our sisters have already achieved when people say to us that women are no good at organizing themselves.

Women last century fought to change marriage laws which gave women no rights to their own earnings and few rights to even visit their children without their husband's permission. They fought for changes in schools, in workhouses and in prisons, and struggled with employers over wages and conditions. They spoke out in public, in spite of the disapproval they met from the majority of the population for daring to leave their own firesides – if they were lucky enough to have one. They came out on strike and showed the same ability as men to organize during a dispute, despite heavier domestic responsibilites. They fought for the right to learn about birth control, and against victimization of women in the early attempts to stamp out venereal disease – when any woman, but no men, could be forced to undergo medical examination and treatment.

This century women have fought for the vote, to be allowed access to education, and for increased control over their own bodies, from birth control to the right to choose abortion. Divorce laws have gradually been changed, although divorce in Scotland remains an expensive and lengthy business, and rights in marriage are still different for men and women. In the two World Wars women have done 'mens' work' – and it has turned out to be possible for public funds to be used for childcare, community kitchens and laundries, taking housework out of the home when women have been needed for other jobs.

Women have fought for – and in some cases won – equal pay and an end to sex discrimination at work. Women have begun to enter public life and women have fought for changes in attitudes to the family and who should do what in the home. There are outstanding personalities in all these struggles and many women whose names are not recorded in the history books have been crucial in organizing local campaigns, supplying information, providing support, raising funds, and arguing causes in the home, the workplace, the tenants' association, parents' organizations and the trade unions. This is not a history book, but it is important to say that women have played a real part in changing our society – and that we don't seem to hear very much about women's achievements.

If you want to read more about women's achievements, try Shiela Rowbotham's *Hidden from History* in which she describes how many historians have ignored the history made by women, and by working women in particular. Sarah Boston's book *Women Workers and the Trade Unions* looks at women's struggles in the trade union movement and gives lots of examples of the efforts, successful and unsuccessful, made by women to improve the unions – as well as some awful stories of the obstructions men have put in the way of women's organization over more than a century – not through malice, but through a genuine belief that they were acting in the interests of trade unionism.

There's real stirring stuff to be read about the suffragettes – particularly those who were socialists too. Sylvia Pankhurst's own accounts of the suffragette struggles and of women's lives during the First World War come alive with her obvious commitment to women, and especially to working women; they also show how good organization and mass popular support led to enormous demonstrations – not many causes can bring half a million people to Hyde Park nowadays!

Other women like Emma Paterson and Mary MacArthur played key roles in organizing women workers. Middle class women fought for entry to the medical profession and set up schools and colleges for girls. Ask your library to help you find books about these women – or better still, ask if they have any records of local women's efforts – in the struggle for the vote, for birth control, for childcare, for schools, or in trade union struggles.

Why bother with all this history? You may find it an inspiration in itself, and it also provides you with plenty of ready answers when people tell you women have never achieved anything, or when you wonder whether women will ever really get anywhere. History also shows us the ways in which some ideas have worked and some struggles have been successful. We can't just copy what others have done in the past – we must work out our own answers – but we can learn from their experiences, when we are planning what to do ourselves.

## Sorting out our priorities

Women *can* fight effectively for their rights. What should we be doing now? What priorities should we have for action when there is so much to be done?

*Unemployment* must be a major problem for all trade unionists at the beginning of the 1980s. Women's unemployment stood at 6 per cent in official Department of Employment figures for August 1980 and although this compares with 9 per cent for men, even the DE says its figures must underestimate women's unemployment because of the large number of women – they estimate 175,000 – who do not register as unemployed. This estimate itself is almost certainly on the low side, but even the official figures show a particularly worrying trend. While in 1980 three men were unemployed for every two who were unemployed in 1975, six women were unemployed in 1980 for every two unemployed in 1975. Female unemployment is rising faster than male unemployment and if new technology has the impact on office jobs which is being predicted yet more women's jobs will go. Part-time workers are also especially vulnerable – and they again are usually women.

*Low pay* remains a problem for women, with women's earning now falling back in relation to men's. Even though this problem has been around as long as the trade unions we can't afford to ignore it.

*Domestic responsibilities* still affect the position of women both at work and in the trade unions. Cutbacks in social services push more women back into the home both as a result of lost jobs as cleaners, teachers, school meals workers, and workers in old peoples' homes and hospitals, and also as a result of lost services and the need to care for the young, the elderly and the sick 'in the community' as official jargon puts it, in the home, in fact. Cutbacks form a nice contrast with wartime demands for women's labour. The TUC Women's Advisory Committee in 1943 commented:

Furthermore, as the demands made upon women by the war have increased, it has been necessary for the State to take responsibility for the establishment of public services to cover work which has hitherto been confined to the home – they have included communal feeding, the setting up of nurseries, the provision of school meals

165

on a larger scale, factory canteens etc . . . The Women's Advisory Committee favours the continuation and extension of these services.

*The law affecting women at work* is far from perfect. The Equal Pay Act and Sex Discrimination Act don't work properly. Maternity rights are more limited than almost anywhere else in Europe. The old protective legislation covering hours of work and health hazards for women is a mess and needs to be rewritten to give improved rights to women workers and to men. Tax law and the whole National Insurance system blatantly treat men and women differently, and rely heavily on the idea of a male breadwinner with female and child dependants – an idea which no longer matches up to reality. Pensions from the state can be criticized in the same way.

*Education and training for jobs* are still given to boys and girls in a different overall pattern, although on paper it may sometimes be possible to show that boys and girls get equal opportunities. Retraining for women returning to paid work is also needed.

*Trade union organization* must be a key area for action. Should we try to win men's interest in issues which affect women or concentrate on organizing women more effectively so that we ourselves can fight better for our own interests – and hope men get the idea from what we are doing? How do we organize women better anyway? What kinds of positive action might work?

## Action at the workplace or change in society?

Another crucial question is whether we can solve the problems which face women at work through the trade unions at all. Are our problems at work only one aspect of our exploitation in society as a whole? Can trade unions step outside the workplace and start to fight for change in women's lives? Do we need other kinds of organization – women's groups, political groups, local groups – to help us fight for change?

Women workers will face new attacks in the next few

years. Unless we organize effectively we can expect to be defeated. If trade unions *can* respond to the needs of women workers and maintain unity and solidarity, trade union organization as a whole will benefit; if women workers can be picked off and defeated without genuine trade union backing the scene is set for a major defeat for everyone in the unions.

This is not something that can be decided by trade union leaders alone. It is up to us, the members of trade unions, to discuss and decide policy, improve our organization and set our priorities. No one else is going to do it for us. We have to start taking the steps to do it ourselves.

# Further reading

Many of the books and pamphlets listed at the end of Chapter four are relevant to this chapter too. *Hear this Brother, Organizing Women Workers, Women, Work and Trade Union Organization,* and *Women Workers and the Trade Unions* are particularly relevant. *My Song is my Own,* listed at the end of Chapter one, is also interesting from a historical point of view. Equal Opportunities Commission literature (address at end of Chapter two) is often concerned with positive action too.

*Hidden from History: Three hundred years of women's oppression and the fight against it* Sheila Rowbotham (Pluto Press, 1977) is still the best introduction to the history that we women have lost because no one thought it was very important to remember what women did. As this really worthwhile book shows women did do a lot, both in trade unions and in other organizations.

*The Suffragette Movement: an intimate account of persons and ideals* Sylvia Pankhurst (Virago, 1977) is a new edition of a book written at the time about the suffragette struggles. Even the old-fashioned style helps to take you back to what it felt like for the women who were involved in the struggle for the vote. This is one of many individual accounts of women's struggles around the turn of the century.

*Spare Rib* is a feminist magazine which you will now find in quite a few newsagents. It gives you up-to-date information on women's strikes, legal cases, and a wide range of other issues in which women are involved.

*Women's Voice* is a bit harder to come by, and gives a bit more emphasis to women at work, though it covers similar areas.

This is not really further reading as such, but do go and look in your local museums. You may find they have interesting collections of material, either about the labour movement in your area or about women's struggles. You may be lucky enough to live near a museum which specializes in working-class history. There is one in East London which has quite a few original magazines, banners, badges from the women's movement, and the People's Palace in Glasgow has a fine display about the Scottish suffragettes. If you really get hooked, go to the Fawcett Library in London, where there is a basement full of all kinds of material relating to over a hundred years of women's fight, with enthusiastic librarians who will help you find what you want. There's no shortage of things to read!

# Index

Chris Baker and Peter Caldwell
**Unions and Change since 1945** £1.75

This volume examines changes within union membership and
union organization, as well as developments in the economic,
political and social environment caused by union activity, with
their implications for the present and the future. The contents
cover:

- how unions have changed since the war
- the extent of union influence on government policy
- the main problems facing unions in the 1980s
- the constraints on union power at work, in society and from
  the government.

Dave Eva and Ron Oswald
**Health and Safety at Work** £1.75

Concentrating on developing an overall view of the relationship
between employers, workers, unions and health and safety
considerations at work, this volume examines:

- the main work hazards and risks
- whether governments and employers are doing enough to
  improve health and safety
- the practical action that union members and representatives
  can take
- likely developments in the future.

The book aims to show that the unions' relatively poor record
concerning health and safety is being reversed, and argues for
collective action as the only way for workers to improve working
conditions.

## Reference, Language and Information

| | | |
|---|---|---|
| ☐ North-South | Brandt Commission | £1.95p |
| ☐ Trachtenberg Speed System of Basic Mathematics | A. Cutler and R. McShane | £1.25p |
| ☐ One-Parent Families | Diana Davenport | 85p |
| ☐ Save It! The Energy Consumer's Handbook | Gary Hammond, Kevin Newport and Carol Russell | £1.25p |
| ☐ Mathematics for the Million | L. Hogben | £1.95p |
| ☐ Militant Islam | Godfrey Jansen | £1.25p |
| ☐ The State of the World Atlas | Michael Kidron and Ronald Segal | £5.95p |
| ☐ Practical Statistics | R. Langley | £1.95p |
| ☐ A Guide to Speaking in Public | Robert Seton Lawrence | 85p |
| ☐ How to Study | H. Maddox | £1.50p |
| ☐ Dictionary of Life Sciences | E. A. Martin | £1.95p |
| ☐ Your Guide to the Law | ed. Michael Molyneux | £3.50p |
| ☐ Getting the Right Job | Chris Parsons and | 80p |
| ☐ Work for Yourself | Angela Neustatter | £1.25p |
| ☐ The Modern Crossword Dictionary | Norman Pulsford | £1.95p |
| ☐ Understanding Poetry | James Reeves | 90p |
| ☐ English Proverbs Explained | | £1.25p |
| ☐ Pan Spelling Dictionary | Ronald Ridout | £1.50p |
| ☐ Career Choice | Audrey Segal | £2.95p |
| ☐ Names for Boys and Girls | L. Sleigh and C. Johnson | £1.50p |
| ☐ Straight and Crooked Thinking | R. H. Thouless | £1.00p |
| ☐ The Best English | G. H. Vallins | 80p |
| ☐ Better English | | 80p |
| ☐ Cassell's Compact Spanish-English, English-Spanish Dictionary | | £1.50p |
| ☐ Dictionary of Earth Sciences | | £1.95p |
| ☐ Dictionary of Economics and Commerce | | £1.50p |
| ☐ Dictionary of Philosophy | | £1.95p |
| ☐ Dictionary of Physical Sciences | | £1.95p |
| ☐ Everyman's Roget's Thesaurus | | £1.95p |
| ☐ Harrap's New Pocket French and English Dictionary | | £1.95p |

| | | | |
|---|---|---|---|
| ☐ | The Limits to Growth | | £1.50p |
| ☐ | Multilingual Commercial Dictionary | | £1.95p |
| ☐ | Pan Dictionary of Synonyms and Antonyms | | £1.95p |
| ☐ | Pan English Dictionary | | £2.50p |
| ☐ | Universal Encyclopaedia of Mathematics | | £2.95p |

Literature Guides

| | | | |
|---|---|---|---|
| ☐ | An Introduction to Shakespeare and his Contemporaries | Marguerite Alexander | £1.50p |
| ☐ | An Introduction to Fifty American Poets | Peter Jones | £1.75p |
| ☐ | An Introduction to Fifty American Novels | Ian Ousby | £1.95p |
| ☐ | An Introduction to Fifty British Novels 1600-1900 | Gilbert Phelps | £2.50p |
| ☐ | An Introduction to Fifty British Poets 1300-1900 | | |
| ☐ | An Introduction to Fifty Modern British Poets | Michael Schmidt | £1.95p £1.50p |
| ☐ | An Introduction to Fifty European Novels | Martin Seymour-Smith | £1.95p |
| ☐ | An Intrdouction to Fifty British Plays 1660-1900 | John Cargill Thompson | £1.95p |

All these books are available at your local bookshop or newsagent, or can be ordered direct from the publisher. Indicate the number of copies required and fill in the form below                                                    3

Name_____
(block letters please)

Address_____

Send to Pan Books (CS Department), Cavaye Place, London SW10 9PG
Please enclose remittance to the value of the cover price plus:

25p for the first book plus 10p per copy for each additional book ordered
to a maximum charge of £1.05 to cover postage and packing
Applicable only in the UK

While every effort is made to keep prices low, it is sometimes
necessary to increase prices at short notice. Pan Books reserve
the right to show on covers and charge new retail prices which
may differ from those advertised in the text or elsewhere